CHARITY DETOX

CHARITY DETOX

What Charity Would Look Like
If We Cared About Results

ROBERT D. LUPTON

HarperOne
An Imprint of HarperCollinsPublishers

HarperOne

Some names have been changed to protect people's privacy.

HarperCollins books may be purchased for educational, business, or sales promotional use. For information please e-mail the Special Markets Department at SPsales@harpercollins.com.

HarperCollins website: http://www.harpercollins.com

HarperCollins®, ■®, and HarperOne™ are trademarks of Harper-Collins Publishers.

FIRST EDITION

Library of Congress Cataloging-in-Publication Data
Lupton, Robert D.
    Charity detox : what charity would look like if we cared about results
/ Robert D. Lupton.
    pages cm
    ISBN 978-0-06-230726-2
 1. Church charities. 2. Charities—Moral and ethical aspects.
 3. Community development—Religious aspects—Christianity.
 4. Social service—Religious aspects—Christianity. I. Title.
    HV530.L867   2015
361.7'5—dc23   2015001456

15 16 17 18 19   RRD(H)   10 9 8 7 6 5 4 3 2 1

CONTENTS

CHARITY DETOX

CHAPTER ONE

The Bad News About Good Works

CHARITY OFTEN HURTS THE PEOPLE it was designed to help. No, I am not a right-wing lobbyist or think-tank libertarian. I am an urban activist who has worked with poor people for over four decades. This fact, that most non-crisis-specific charity is harmful, serves as an indictment of the field I work in, and so it is with a heaviness of heart that I report this sad and surprising truth. In 2011, I wrote *Toxic Charity* to shine the light of real-life experience on the largely unexamined impacts of philanthropy and aid. It was not my intention to offend generous givers; nor did I want to discourage kindhearted volunteers. But it was high time, I felt, for someone to admit the truth about a highly popular practice that was yielding troubling unintended consequences. I wasn't being unkind. I was just being honest. And I felt we should be doing much, much better than we were (and are currently) doing.

As a seasoned practitioner in community development work, I have witnessed firsthand how food, clothing, and money given to assist those in need more often than not produce unhealthy dependency and end up harming those the donation was intended to help. After four decades of living and serving among the poor—decades spent coordinating hundreds of volunteer service projects and watching well-intentioned volunteers do for my neighbors what my neighbors should be doing for themselves—I felt it was finally time to take the risk of going public with the dirty little secret that on-the-ground charity workers know all too well but are loath to admit. The hard reality is that it takes more than compassionate hearts and generous gifts to elevate people in need out of poverty. In fact, giving to people in need what they could be gaining from their own initiative may well be the kindest way to destroy them.

My 2011 exposé stirred up considerable controversy. People were surprised by my news. How could any reasonable person claim that charity does more harm than good? How could anyone argue that a hot meal and a clean bed are harmful to a hungry homeless man shivering in the cold? Or that a hot shower and a fresh change of clothes could be anything but beneficial to a woman who has been sleeping under a bridge? To even suggest such things, some people charged, was akin to suggesting that loving one's neighbor is a bad idea. Some even accused me of sabotaging the noble—indeed, biblical—cause of caring for the poor.

While I was hoping to create a lively discussion by writing *Toxic Charity*, I didn't write it to stir up controversy. More than ever, I stand behind the surprising truths I uncovered, not just during the writing of the book, but during my decades of work both with the poor and with charities and ministries that genuinely want to serve and make a difference in the lives of others. The fact is, we cannot serve others out of poverty, no matter how much we may want to. That is a core concept of both my mission and this book. And the reason I am so passionate about broadcasting this bad news about the status quo is that I care deeply about charity's goals and results: I want to move people out of poverty. That is my life's work.

My calling first led me to found Family Consultation Service (FCS), an Atlanta-based nonprofit focused on the needs of inner-city youth and families in the community I came to call home. Over time the mission of FCS expanded into transforming entire urban neighborhoods, and its name was changed to Focused Community Strategies to more accurately describe its work. My commitment to moving people out of poverty then took me farther afield as I became an active board member of Opportunity Nicaragua and applied the principles learned in the United States' urban experience to a developing country.

The insights I have learned through this work—through project after project both here and abroad—are counterintuitive. The truths I have learned are counterintuitive. For example, I believe now, as I did when I wrote *Toxic Charity*, that the only effective charity is the kind that asks *more* from those being served, rather than less. Asking for more sends an affirming message to the recipient that he or she also has something of value to offer.

It's easy to get discouraged about all the poverty in the world. After all, Christ himself said, "The poor you will always have with you" (Matthew 26:11 and elsewhere). As a result, we may feel helpless in the face of trying to solve the problem of global destitution. But in this book, I will offer inspiring new avenues that are open to us for making true and lasting change, especially through the use of social enterprise. This exciting shift from the traditional dynamic of charitable giving is a powerful weapon in the war against poverty.

In other words, I don't have only bad news to tell you. Many dedicated people who work among the poor are just as frustrated as I am with the non-results of our traditional methods. Many of them are pioneering new models of charity, ones that keep their eyes focused on what truly makes a difference. I will talk about these new models, and how we can support them, throughout this book. Following their lead is how we can best detox our toxic charity.

The work I have done in the past, and much of what I discuss in this book, concerns organizations that work with giving, but I will also outline how you, as an individual, can bring about meaningful change in the world and in the lives of others. This might take the form of teaching what you know about business to someone who can use this knowledge to better his or her life. Or it may mean being a good neighbor—organizing a crime watch, being active in the PTA, and helping transform your community for *everyone* who lives there. Or it could be as simple as using the criteria I develop in this book as a guide to what charities and ministries you support financially. All of us, however, need to detox our charities and learn new rules in order for the results to match our ideals.

The Doctor Will Kill You Now

Is HURTFUL CHARITY BETTER than no charity at all? The answer is no. Take an honest look at the outcomes of our benevolence—from the soup kitchen in inner-city Atlanta to the entire country of Haiti—and the answer becomes obvious. Despite our most charitable efforts, the world's poor are not emerging from poverty. The poverty gap in the United States is increasing; and across the globe, in those lands where our aid is most concentrated, the poor are getting poorer.

I understand how disheartening it can be to discover that one's sincere acts of caring harm the very ones we intended to help. The truth is disturbing, but if the poor are ever to emerge from poverty, we all have to face this truth, regardless of how it makes us feel.

As a sobering example of how entrenched wrong thinking

can be, and why we need to work so hard in order to change our models, consider the eighteenth-century physician. Back then medical doctors were taught that the time-honored practice of bloodletting would help cure sick patients by removing bad or stagnant blood. Unchallenged for more than four thousand years, bloodletting was universally accepted as the most effective remedy for almost every disease. Although it seems archaic today, the prevailing theory before the circulatory system was fully understood was that blood could stagnate in the extremities. A buildup of bad blood was thought to cause all manner of maladies. The cure was to purge.

And everyone bought in. For eons. Ancient cultures like the Mesopotamians and Egyptians. Hippocrates, the father of modern medicine, endorsed bloodletting as an effective treatment. As did Socrates and Plato. The Talmud, the central text of Rabbinic Judaism, specified certain days for bloodletting, while early Christian writings offered advice on which saints' days were most favorable for the practice. Bloodletting was prescribed for everything from cholera to cancer, tetanus to tuberculosis, gout to gangrene. The more blood, the better. In 1799, George Washington, suffering from a throat infection, requested that his physician drain four pints of blood. Not surprisingly, shortly after the procedure, Washington died.

Modern medical advances finally exposed as harmful this once-common practice. Young scientist Louis Pasteur discovered that it was germs, not bad blood, that caused disease. The revelation was a medical game-changer. Imagine the shock experienced by doctors who learned that their attempts to heal had actually harmed or even killed their patients. And yet this misguided model had persisted for four thousand years! That is the power of an entrenched paradigm.

And that is what we are up against when we try to change how we think about charity. Our very models of what it means to be and do good are wrapped up with images of food pantries, homeless shelters, and giveaway programs—despite the fact that no one can show that these efforts help people move out of poverty. Just as doctors did not want to hear that their treatment strategies were not just ineffective but detrimental, neither do charity workers or dedicated volunteers want to hear that their efforts have not only failed to do good but have actually harmed those they wanted to help.

Yes, we have been giving handouts to the poor for thousands of years, but that does not make it an effective strategy for moving people out of poverty—especially now that we have other, proven models that *do* work.

Recently, I explained the harm of toxic charity to a very active civic group. They had organized a large-scale gardening initiative to grow fresh produce, which they then gave to their city's homeless. Though their work was rightly motivated, the initiative was fostering unhealthy dependency. I suggested that they "detoxify" their program by involving the recipients in the growing process—a proposal that was clearly unwelcome.

When I suggested that the positive feelings the civic group

received from their participation was at the heart of their program, rather than its effectiveness in helping the homeless, I got this response from one of the coordinators: "This is a lot of work. I would have quit a long time ago if there weren't so many hungry people. If I wanted to feel good, I'd be sitting on the beach with a book." In his mind, the program simply *had* to be right—look how hard volunteers were working.

Resistance is an understandable reaction to new insights, especially when they call into question traditional methods of care. But resistance can also hinder the discovery of more effective ways to serve. Worse than resistance, however, is *denial*. Denial is failing to admit—to even *consider*—that a method of treatment may actually be causing harm.

Just Following God's Orders

UNFORTUNATELY, ONE OF THE most powerful drivers of American compassion is one of its greatest abusers. American churches are at the forefront of the burgeoning compassion industry, spending billions on dependency-producing food pantries, clothes closets, service projects, and mission trips that serve mainly themselves and inadvertently turn people into beggars. Unexamined charity—charity that fails to ask the hard questions about outcomes—only perpetuates poverty, despite its best intentions. As megachurch pastor Rick Warren states in his foreword to Wayne Grudem and Barry

Asmus's *The Poverty of Nations*, "Having traveled the globe for thirty years and trained leaders in 164 countries, I've witnessed firsthand that almost every government and NGO (nonprofit) poverty program is actually harmful to the poor, hurting them in the long run rather than helping them. The typical poverty program creates dependency, robs people of dignity, stifles initiative, and can foster a 'What have you done for me lately?' sense of entitlement."

Responsible charity, on the other hand, engages not only the heart but the mind as well. One of the most significant, rational decisions that determine the outcome of our charity is distinguishing between *crisis* and *chronic need*. In times of crisis, an immediate emergency intervention is required. When an earthquake devastates Haiti, for example, an emergency response is the right—and only—response. Food, water, shelter, and medical supplies are essential to save lives. But when the bleeding has stopped, when emergency supplies have been distributed, when people are housed in temporary shelters, it is time for rebuilding to begin. The strategy of crisis intervention must then shift to a strategy of development.

And herein lies the problem. It is far easier to raise money and mobilize volunteers for emergency assistance than it is to plan and execute the long, painstaking process of rebuilding lives. Thus agencies and volunteers tend to remain in relief mode long after the transition to development should have taken place. When crisis intervention persists beyond the crisis, it produces diminishing returns.

Much of the giving in America is misplaced. We respond generously to stories of people in crisis, but in fact most of our charity goes to people who face predictable, solvable problems of chronic poverty. An emergency response to chronic need is at best counterproductive and, over time, is actually harmful.

Take hunger, for example. Is it a crisis, or is it a chronic issue? Well, that depends. When a famine sweeps sub-Saharan Africa, starvation is a life-and-death crisis. But in urban America, hunger is a chronic issue, not a crisis. In urban America, we do not have starvation. We have temporary hunger, yes—but not starvation. In my forty-plus years of inner-city work, I have never seen a starving person. I have seen plenty of poor nutrition and food insecurity, but never outright starvation. And yet charities and churches continue to use crisis-intervention strategies that foster dependence. Food pantries and soup kitchens are among the worst offenders. Although they are simply trying to combat hunger, they continue to feed a man a fish, when they really need to teach him how to fish.

Churches may respond, "But isn't serving the poor exactly what Jesus asks us to do?" On the surface, yes: feeding, clothing, and sheltering the poor seems to fulfill Jesus's mandate that we serve him when we serve those most in need (Matthew 25:31–46). Our unconditional giving seems to reflect the unconditional grace we have received from God. A closer look, however, reveals a less redemptive reality. What if such giving is perpetuating unhealthy dependency? What if it's supporting a destructive lifestyle? What if these well-meaning services diminish the dignity of recipients and erode their work ethic? Surely Christ intended the church's compassion to be helpful, not hurtful.

While our motives are noble, our charitable practice is often poor in comparison. The outpouring of compassion from churches and charitable groups in times of calamity is immediate, generous, and effective, a shining attribute of our culture that should, rightfully, make us proud. But our methods of caring for those in chronic poverty, both here and abroad, have been largely counterproductive. Charity that frees the poor from poverty requires a more thoughtful approach—one that is admittedly much more complex and time-consuming, and one that requires far more personal involvement in the lives of those we serve.

Converting to Results-Based Charity

So I ask again, is harmful charity better than no charity at all? We have certainly concluded that *no* medical treatment is better than misinformed malpractice (thank you, Dr. Pasteur). Fortunately, it is beginning to dawn on the world of compassion that the root causes of poverty can be addressed effectively only through development, not through one-way giving. This insight may be as transformative as the medical profession's discovery that blood transfusions, not bloodletting, was a key to curing sick patients.

One organization that is making great strides in restructuring, or what I would call "detoxifying," its charitable endeavors is the Association of Gospel Rescue Missions, which has been helping the homeless in North America since the 1870s. For the first time in their centuries-old history, they are currently reconsidering their free-service policies. At their recent national conferences they have engaged in lively debates about their historic "giveaway" philosophy. New thought leaders are reexamining their "grace is free and so is our service" theology. And new voices are emerging, challenging the organization's old paradigm, arguing instead that "everyone has something to contribute."

Darryl Bartlett runs the Holland Rescue Mission, where he has implemented a "personal development" system to help the homeless population of Holland, Michigan. The results have been extraordinary. In exchange for a free week of lodging and meals, guests are required to contribute in meaningful ways—making up their bed, performing kitchen duty, mopping floors, doing laundry. During their "free" week, guests work closely with a caseworker, who helps them establish a personalized growth plan, manage their finances, and take first steps toward self-sufficiency. Guests also enjoy full access to the facility's laundry room and telephone banks and receive appropriate clothing for job interviews. Guests who demonstrate initiative are invited to stay on longer and enter a job training program that provides real-life employment experience at the mission, a paycheck, and mandatory financial management.

At Holland Rescue Mission, success is measured not by the number of beds filled or meals served, but by the number of guests who "graduate" drug-free, secure stable employment, settle existing debts, move into independent living, and connect with a church or other support group. Word on the street in Holland is: "If you're ready to change, go to the Holland Rescue Mission." It may take a longer commitment with fewer participants, but there is no question that the mission's outcomes have dramatically improved.

Six hundred miles to the south, another Rescue Mission is grappling with change—change not only in their internal program but in how they impact their surrounding neighborhood.

The massive new highway overpass that cuts across downtown Knoxville, Tennessee, creates a cavernous shelter from the elements. Beneath the gigantic concrete-and-steel structure that rumbles day and night with nonstop traffic, hundreds of homeless people congregate. They are attracted by church groups that pull up regularly to distribute their charity. The handouts are as diverse as the imaginations of suburban Christian leaders who tell heartrending stories of women and children shivering in the night, and barefoot men whose feet ooze with raw sores. Blankets, tents, shoes, clean socks, toiletries, and food of all kinds—from hot soup to cold-cut sandwiches to box lunches to chargrilled hamburgers with all the condiments. The overpass has created "compassion central," where the city's most destitute meet the suburbs' most generous.

Within the shadow of the overpass stands a neatly painted complex of connected buildings known to all the area's homeless as Knoxville Area Rescue Ministries (KARM), which houses up to five hundred guests every night. The mission seldom turns anyone away, other than the inebriated and known violent offenders. Despite the numbers, there is order amid the crush of humanity pressing through KARM's doors. All guests receive a computerized identification card to record their presence. Meals prepared by homeless guests are served in orderly shifts. Residents also perform kitchen cleanup, and the mission's many beds are stripped and made up daily by their occupants. Guests who volunteer in the laundry room launder sheets, pillowcases, towels, and washcloths. There seems to be a job for everyone. Some people spend a night or two and then move on. Others stay longer, taking advantage of counseling and classes that prepare them to reenter the job market. "Everybody who really wants help," one resident commented, "can get it here."

Though KARM and "compassion central" occupy adjacent turf, they are worlds apart. The charity convoys of kindhearted church folks that pull up daily under the viaduct—some regularly, most sporadically—offer unconditional compassion to willing recipients who gladly take whatever is being handed out. The grace that is extended has no strings attached. No distinction is made between the mentally ill and the predators who prey upon them. Nor is any thought given to security—for example, the matter of where blankets and shoes and other handouts might be safely kept when recipients go looking for work. Dependencies that are fostered or destructive lifestyles that are enabled are not the concern of these caring purveyors of love. Their grace is free—free from obligation, free from accountability, free from any expectation of reciprocity. It is pure.

But it's not without consequence. Violence frequently erupts among the deranged and intoxicated who push and elbow their way up the handout lines. Police are often called in to break up fights and handcuff instigators. The free handouts are like magnets that draw the needy into a deepening lifestyle of dependency, turning the able-bodied into perpetual beggars. And then there's the unsightly trash: discarded lunch boxes and food wrappers, half-eaten sandwiches and empty beer cans litter the street. Residents and business owners desperate to restore a measure of vitality to the neighborhood complain about the constant mess. Distressing, too, are the panhandlers and vagrants who hang around the area, which creates an unwelcoming if not dangerous atmosphere. "Compassion central" is anything but community-friendly.

KARM, on the other hand, is a model of responsible compassion. Not only is it a good neighbor, but it is also a good friend to those it serves. KARM guests receive the affirming message that everyone has some God-given capacity to help both self and others. *Everyone*. KARM's message is this: The Creator has entrusted to all of us certain abilities that, when rightly employed, align us with our created purpose. That's how we gain our lives. It is not unloving to expect people to do their part. Just the opposite. It is cruel to send the message that a person has nothing of worth to offer. Being needed is the ultimate affirmation of human worth. The compassionate volunteers of "compassion central," in their zeal to help, have tragically missed this fundamental truth.

Slowly but surely, people are starting to figure out that the only effective charity involves much more than a simple handout with nothing required of the recipient. This change in paradigm is symptomatic of a much broader societal shift. Throughout the country, churches are starting to question traditional charity practices. Some are replacing Angel Trees with Christmas stores, and food pantries with food co-ops. Self-sufficiency is now a common consideration in mission strategy.

Foundations, too, are starting to ask hard questions—questions about return on investment (ROI) and measurable outcomes. As a result, many foundations are shifting funds toward programs that can produce evidence of lasting behavioral change, not merely impressive numbers of people served or quantities of commodities distributed.

Such dramatic shifts demonstrate that it's entirely possible to detoxify charities. But there's still more work to do. Since the publication of *Toxic Charity*, I've spoken to hundreds of organizations, both big and small, about detoxifying their programs and charitable endeavors. Nine times out of ten, the first question people ask me is, "How do we start?" *This* book attempts to answer that question.

Moving the Poverty Needle

TO BE POOR IS to be marginalized, isolated from mainstream society, excluded from the privileges and advantages available to the rest of the culture. When people become isolated from and devalued by society, their dignity diminishes; their self-worth erodes. Isolation in inner cities or in rural communities more often than not means substandard education, a severe lack of viable job opportunities, and an almost total absence of upwardly mobile neighbors. Poor communities everywhere are universally plagued by exploitive businesses and a relentless, deadly undertow of criminal influences. When hard work yields only continued poverty, a person understandably abandons his or her ambition; a work ethic loses meaning. And when the pressures of survival take precedence over the motivation to achieve, hope begins to flicker. Resignation is inevitable, and a poverty of spirit begins to take root.

How can we begin to quantify this poverty of spirit? Is there an accurate meter by which to gauge hope? It is certainly not as easy to measure spiritual poverty as it is to track rising and falling income levels or the steady accumulation of material possessions. But we can think of our reserve of economic, social, and spiritual wellness like the gas tank in our car, and we can see, according to the needle on the gauge, where we stand—full or empty. There are factors that can fill the tank: motivation, planning, training, and independence. If strategies to alleviate poverty yield increased drive and focus on future goals, educational advancement, and improved self-sufficiency, we can be reasonably well assured that we are moving the poverty needle in the right direction. Service may temporarily improve the quality of life for individuals being served, but service alone will never empower a community to rise out of poverty. Moving the needle in a positive direction requires a two-pronged approach: economic and community development.

To put it simply, the alleviation of poverty begins with a good job—one that enables a person to adequately support his or her family. While job training remains a legitimate role for nonprofit organizations, the for-profit business world is the ultimate source of sustainable employment. Historically, compassionate service volunteers have responded to human need, usually asking for help from bottom-line businesspeople to support these efforts financially. And yet these same bottom-line businesspeople are seldom engaged to help create solutions to the larger problem, even though their expertise and pragmatism are key to eliminating poverty. A decent job with the potential for advancement and adequate benefits is essential if a family is ever going to escape poverty.

But a decent job will not end poverty in a depressed community. A decent job generally allows an upwardly mobile family to leave their old neighborhood behind, which only compounds that community's isolation and exclusion. What is good for an achieving family is not necessarily good for the neighborhood. When a neighborhood's most capable residents leave, their departure diminishes hope for those remaining behind. If our attempts to open the door of opportunity for individual families increase the pathological effects of poverty, we will have succeeded only in exacerbating the problem. Unless we simultaneously address both the needs of individuals and those of the community, it is unlikely that we will make any headway in alleviating poverty.

Which brings us to the second prong of attack: community development. Healthy communities foster healthy offspring. When the fabric of a community is rewoven with capable neighbor-leaders, when it once again becomes a healthy place for children to grow up, the community then becomes an environment that not only retains its upwardly mobile residents but attracts new ones as well.

Capitalism and the Kingdom

IN JUDEO-CHRISTIAN TEACHING, *shalom* (which means wholeness, prosperity, and peace) is the end to which all righteous people strive, both here and in the hereafter. Associating unbridled capitalism and unfettered job growth with shalom may be tempting, yes, but as a minister friend rightly likes to remind me, "Capitalism could be baptized, but it is not God's final revelation."

But in spite of its bent toward self-interest, even with its excesses and inequities, capitalism has a historic opportunity to create shared wealth that can benefit every person on the globe. I am convinced that our best hope for moving the poverty needle toward financial wellness once and for all lies in the best practices of the free market. Does this mean that capitalism is the divine design for bringing about shalom? I suspect not. Nor is *any* economic system devised by flawed humanity. What capitalism needs in order to fulfill its promise is concentrated compassion, or something I like to refer to as sanctified self-interest.

Dylan and Anna Wilk are prime examples of this trait. By the time Dylan had reached his twenty-fifth birthday, he was already tired of success. His interest in computer games had turned into a multimillion-dollar enterprise, one of the largest computer game suppliers in the United Kingdom. Celebrated as one of Britain's rising business stars, he was well on his way to becoming a major player in a burgeoning global market. As quoted by Thomas Graham in *The Philippine Star*, Dylan admitted, "The obsession with profit didn't bring out the best in me" ("Social Business Summit: No Ordinary Love Story," updated September 8, 2013). So he cashed in his chips and ventured out into an unexplored world to find more meaning in life.

He found more than he bargained for when he landed in the Philippines. Not only was his imagination captivated by an amazing faith-based community development project he discovered among the poorest rural villages, but his heart was captured by a beautiful Filipina named Anna Meloto, who just happened to be the daughter of the movement's leader. They married and the two of them joined the Gawad Kalinga ("Give Care") community development effort.

Later, on a visit to the United States, Anna noticed that natural health and beauty products were marketed to middle-class Americans at very reasonable prices, while only elite Filipinas could afford them back home. The fact that these products had to be imported in the island nation raised their cost tremendously. Dylan and Anna realized, upon checking out the ingredients, that most of them could easily be grown in the Philippines. If the villagers could be persuaded to grow the raw materials, and if Dylan were to reengage his business skills, perhaps they could together establish a cosmetic company that would provide good jobs for people there.

They launched Human Nature in a cramped room with, according to Dylan, "zero marketing budget." In four years, the company has emerged as the leading beauty and cosmetic brand in the Philippines. All products are made with natural ingredients and are sourced, whenever possible, in the Philippines. Human Nature—whose motto is "Pro-Philippines, pro-poor, pro-environment"—buys directly from local growers, which cuts out the intermediaries and allows the company to sell its products at affordable rates. Some rural communities have since established processing plants that create added value and additional employment. In addition to training local residents in farming techniques, basic record keeping, and financial projections, Human Nature provides equipment and technical support to make sure they can maximize the profits they generate.

Dylan and Anna are on a mission. They want to eliminate poverty from their country, a land where 90 percent of the population lives on less than two dollars a day. "Now, more than ever," says Anna, "business should be at the forefront of addressing social and environmental issues because it has the resources, technology, and discipline to make a significant impact. All it needs is the heart and will to do so."

To Dylan and Anna, people matter as much as profits, and they demonstrate this by paying their employees an "ethical wage," which means narrowing the typical income gap between owners and workers. They provide benefits as well. "When workers are in need here," Dylan said in Graham's article, "it is often only the employer who can help them. So at Human Nature we started to realize that the way business is done could have a profound impact on the country. Business has more money than the government, and yet we often think that only government has the responsibility to make life better for our people. If we convince lots of business owners to make small changes, then it will have a far bigger impact than what we can achieve as an individual business."

Creating economic opportunities and transforming communities may seem like daunting challenges for churches and charities to undertake, particularly when some of their practices and giving infrastructures have been in place for years. And, admittedly, this undertaking does call for a significant shift from the way we have historically conducted service. But it is not rocket science. Remember the Association of Gospel Rescue Missions. They are successfully overhauling a system that they have been using for more than a century. Think about Dylan and Anna Wilk. They successfully applied good business practices to the practice of doing good. Like Rescue Missions and Human Nature, hundreds of other organizations and businesses are currently doing the same thing—all because they've figured out how to "detoxify" their charitable practices.

In the following pages, I will explain how to do the same thing, both in theory and in practice. The first part of the book highlights specific for-profit models of operation, while simultaneously sharing example after example of creative, entrepreneurial visionaries developing new "technologies of compassion" that have produced remarkable results around the world. Building upon these new strategies and examples, later chapters feature even more inspiring stories of organizations and businesses that are successfully solving poverty and its attendant problems—from hunger and community rehabilitation to education, economic reform, and international development—through the very same practices that constitute a successful business. These real-life examples offer practical illustrations of the myriad ways a new generation of peacemakers, pacesetters, and partners are applying these principles in parishes and towns from Atlanta to Nairobi, from Brooklyn to Choluteca.

This is a hopeful moment, an exciting time for innovators and compassion workers alike. My hope is that one of the following examples will inspire you to implement a similar approach in order to undergo a complete charity detox and accelerate, once and for all, a lasting and positive change.

CHAPTER TWO

Partnering with Business

I HAVE NEVER PLACED A political campaign sign in my yard. Not that I'm uninterested in who gets elected to public office. That's clearly important to me. But going public with my political biases would be likely to alienate about half the supporters of my nonprofit, Focused Community Strategies. It's better for business, I have found, to keep my political opinions to myself, to talk out of both sides of my mouth when necessary, and to keep my mouth shut when in doubt.

Some might call me spineless. I prefer diplomatic. I can usually see both sides of an issue, and, when I can find common ground between differing opinions, I do my best to steer the conversation toward mutual understanding. When that doesn't work, I try to offer a conciliatory comment and then change the subject.

There is one subject, though, that I have always been very straight about: caring for the poor. This is a conviction. There may be disagreement about how best to do this caring, but compassionate and just treatment of the poor is nonnegotiable. It is a divine mandate. And I will go to the mat over this one. Because I have been politically elusive, my Democratic friends often pigeonhole me as a Republican with a big heart. My Republican friends peg me as a Democrat opposed to entitlements. Both camps consider me an anomaly. That's probably good for keeping diverse friends and satisfied supporters.

But after forty-plus years of living and serving among the poor, I have witnessed nearly every expression of care that good people have visited upon the less fortunate—from feeding the homeless, to counseling pregnant girls to keep their babies, to patching widows' roofs, to advocating for addicts who need treatment. I have done all of these and hundreds more acts of kindness. And I have been joined by countless others whose hearts compel them to help those in need. Sometimes our service has made a difference. Sometimes we have inflicted unintentional harm. One thing I am quite sure of, however, is that it's much safer being a supportive listener than being an eager helper. And another thing I have learned: when you do for others what they have the capacity to do for themselves, you are likely doing them a disservice.

After four decades of service, the romance is gone. I am left with an unvarnished view of the realities of urban poverty. But the divine calling imposed upon me to become a neighbor to the poor has never been lifted. And because my commitment and voice and heart remain on the side of the poor, my Democratic friends want to embrace me as a fellow liberal, although one with a few right-wing tendencies! And because I have seen the destructive effects of subsidizing poverty and oppose dependency-producing entitlements, I am accepted by Republican friends as a fellow conservative, although one with a bleeding heart.

Ever since I came out of the closet with *Toxic Charity*, however, I fear that maintaining this delicate balance is beginning to be perceived as a "list to the starboard," or tilt to the right. But all I'm doing is paying attention to what actually moves people out of poverty. I have begun to publicly declare that the only thing that will enable the poor to emerge from poverty is a decent job. And the primary creators of decent jobs are businesspeople who believe deeply in the free-enterprise system.

For-profits and not-for-profits represent two fundamental divisions of our economy: wealth creation and wealth transfer. Business is the wealth creator; the rest of the economy operates on the transfer of that wealth. I began to realize how strange it was that business creators, so essential to our well-being, are so often viewed as somehow less spiritual, less compassionate than those who live off the wealth those businesspeople produce! Strange, too, how we esteem sacrificial nonprofit "servants" but malign as greedy capitalists the for-profit producers who underwrite their charities. Why are people in my line of work so comfortable seeing these two groups in such contrast-ing ways?

As I have said before, I have become convinced that the only thing that will enable the poor to emerge from pov-erty is a decent job. I am further convinced that free-market capitalists—the so-called wealth creators—offer the best chance of creating decent jobs. You can't *serve* a community out of poverty. Don't get me wrong—services are impor-tant. A first-rate school, quality health care, vibrant churches, abundant parks and recreation, good city services—these are characteristics of a healthy community. They are very impor-tant. But they are not sufficient. They are all by-products of a healthy economy. Without a viable economy, communities will not prosper.

For some reason, the religious and social service sectors often seem to miss this. They have somehow overlooked the fact that it is business that creates the wealth that funds all our human service governmental/cultural/religious/educational institutions. Wealth-creating industries (historically, fish-ing, farming, mining, and manufacturing) are the wellsprings from which our employment and quality of life emerge. Our churches, hospitals, universities, libraries, art centers—marks of a prosperous nation—exist only because we are blessed with an abundance of business entrepreneurs and a land rich with resources (and, of course, a stable government). We can build interstate highways, create city-center parks, equip a top-notch military, all thanks to our wealth-producing business class. Our mission trips, our community service projects, our donated food and clothing surpluses—all our charitable efforts—are made possible by those who every day risk their resources in the marketplace.

Do I sound too much like a right-wing capitalist? Perhaps. But what I have learned comes out of decades of wrestling with the problem of what really moves people out of poverty. I don't care about political and cultural labels. I care about results.

Charity's Bottom Line

A GROUP OF SUCCESSFUL business leaders recently met in Chicago for a two-day economic development summit with urban ministry leaders from across the country. Everyone at the gathering was involved in business in one way or another. Most of us were running nonprofit businesses—business-as-ministry enterprises to create jobs for unemployed residents in our depressed neighborhoods. Only a handful of the participants were for-profit business owners. During the course of candid, sometimes confrontational discussions, it became apparent that the nonprofit operations were far more ministry-minded than the profit-motivated enterprises. As a matter of fact, none of the nonprofit businesses was turning a profit—all were being subsidized in one form or another. The primary vision that drove these enterprises was job creation and the services they provided to the community.

"This isn't economic development!" one of the for-profit guys declared. "This is social service. To develop the economy of a community, there must be wealth-creating enterprises, which require profit generation." He was right. At best, nonprofits have a symbiotic relationship with the wealth-generating world. At worst, this relationship is parasitic. "Social services are important," the for-profit guy affirmed, "but don't call what they do economic development." Job training and job experience are certainly helpful to the individuals being employed—maybe even life-giving. Ultimately, though, they exist only because the upstream wealth-creating community supports them. (As I said, this was a rather candid discussion.)

The nonprofit participants confessed their ambivalence about making money "on the backs of the poor." They leaned decidedly toward justice and equality. The disparity of wages between owners and workers troubled them. For many in our group, profit was suspect, coupled closely with greed. Wealth was seen as seductive, a slippery slope toward privilege and self-indulgence. Unlike our business-owner participants, who viewed profit as essential, good, and highly motivating, the nonprofit folks saw it as dangerous if not immoral.

After two days of vigorous debate, however, both camps began to expand their perspectives and arrived at similar conclusions. We all agreed that wealth creation is the bedrock of economic vitality for any community, whether we like to admit it or not. Similarly, we all agreed that a healthy community needs both nonprofits and for-profits—both human services and wealth generators—but that profit making should be reserved for the business sector, while social services work best in the hands of nonprofits. Finally, we all agreed that true economic development is impossible without both.

There's no way around it: economies are built on trade. From the earliest records of human life, exchange has been essential to survival. Hunters calculate the worth of a deer based on how much the meat, hide, and antlers will bring from the village butcher, tanner, and implement-maker. Farmers toil in the fields in the hope of producing a harvest that will yield enough at the market to supply their families with adequate clothing and shelter. Quilters, long after their children are in bed, work by candlelight to fashion quilts they will later barter for dishes and pottery to beautify their homes. Exchange is how communities and nations flourish.

Trade accelerates wealth exponentially. It builds upon the skills of its diverse participants. The carpenter's adeptness is enhanced by practice. He devises tools and techniques to increase his productivity and quality. Demand for his furniture rises with his proficiency. The same is true of the blacksmith and the baker and the seamstress. In this creative process of exchange, both talent and wealth increase.

An economically healthy community (and nation) employs all of its able-bodied workers. Some raise livestock; some mine coal; some teach children; some run hardware stores. And in this wonderfully complex process of exchange, everyone assumes a needed function. Everyone contributes. Kids deliver newspapers; teenagers babysit; seniors do mailings for the church. A healthy society is a working society.

Problems arise when some people can find no productive outlet for their labor. "Idle hands are the devil's workshop," as Grandma used to say. Unemployed young men hanging out on the street corner are an unhealthy sign. It is equally unhealthy for welfare recipients to sit on the stoop waiting for their checks to arrive. Unhealthy for society, unhealthy for idle individuals. When one is unneeded in the workforce, self-worth takes a hit. Alternative sources of income and self-esteem are sought. Illicit economies begin to take root. Antisocial behavior increases. Life loses value. A culture of "expendables" turns destructive, both to itself and to society.

Subsidizing inactivity is a bad practice. Yes, people have to survive. But they will not thrive if they are induced by charity (public or private, government or religious) to be unproductive. Purposeful work is what establishes one's place in society. In addition to providing legitimate income, work is what gives one purpose, enables one to develop a skill, earns one a positive reputation.

How inspiring it was to hear accounts of employees of companies hit hard by the Great Recession who elected to take reduced hours and wages in order to avoid layoffs of fellow workers! Are there not similar stories yet to be told of churches that created jobs instead of benevolence handouts for the unemployed who come to their doors for assistance? And businesspeople who invested their time helping a struggling inner-city entrepreneur launch a successful catering business? And a Sunday school class who committed their weekly collection toward employing a welfare mom at a thrift store in her community?

Heartwarming stories of aid that do *not* end with the recipient productively engaged in meaningful exchange are emotional deceptions. Trade is God's design for a healthy, interdependent community. It is a gift. As the ancient Hebrew Talmud states, the highest form of charity is to anonymously provide a man or a woman employment; the lowest is to directly offer him or her aid.

Perhaps, then, it is time to revisit our wealth-disparaging theologies and reintroduce a righteous respect for the God-ordained capacity for wealth creation. So fearful have we become of the dangers of mammon that we have forgotten that a flourishing economy is a reflection of God's universal grace. At the very least, let's admit to ourselves that nonprofits alone will never move a community out of poverty. If done well, they can improve the quality of life—health care, education, religious life, to cite a few examples—but they do not ultimately enable a people to thrive. Only for-profit businesses produce enough wealth to create enough jobs to lift a community out of poverty. If the poverty needle is to move in a positive direction, that mission ultimately lies with the wealth creators.

The Power of Self-Interest

Take my friend Bill Mallory, for example. His successful import business was growing, but he was frequently frustrated by quality-control issues and unpredictable shipping schedules from his Pacific Rim suppliers. He finally decided to set up his own manufacturing operation in the Philippines and produce his own line of garden and outdoor products. He and his wife, Page, relocated to Cebu, set up a small production facility near an outlying village, hired locals at a fair wage, and began producing and shipping quality products.

But troubling problems that impeded production soon arose. Employees were taking far too many sick days, and many were showing up at work with a high fever and severe shakes. A physician informed Bill and Page that most of the tropical illnesses plaguing his employees could be remedied by inexpensive antibiotics and a daily dose of vitamins. In a decision that was both pragmatic and compassionate, Bill ordered bulk supplies of the needed medicines and hired a nurse to dispense personal health care to his workforce. Page handed out vitamins and hugs. Production stabilized. Profits increased.

It is enlightened self-interest to keep a healthy, motivated workforce. Recognizing this, Bill provides health insurance for all his employees and on occasion gives outright gifts to workers who require hospitalization or procedures not covered by insurance. He gives educational bonuses so that all employees' children can attend school through high school.

He runs a learning center for preschoolers at the factory. He shares company profits through regular bonuses. He conducts optional weekly Bible studies on company time. He has funded the start-up of three churches and a training center for pastors. And profits continue to grow. In fact, his business is now the seventh-largest exporter in Cebu.

Bill now has three plants. He employs three thousand workers at peak production periods. His business has spawned more than fifty ancillary businesses that have created an additional three thousand jobs in the area. The economy of the region is improving measurably. The poverty needle is moving in a positive direction. "We've created a lot of jobs," Bill says. "We have shown the manufacturing community that you can run a business, pay the legal wage, pay government extras, not overwork the workers, treat them as partners and family, and still be successful. Others are starting to follow the model."

Bill is doing well and doing good at the same time. While he would without hesitation tell you that his company is dedicated to God, that he sees his work as a ministry, he would also be quick to admit that he is a significant beneficiary of this wealth-producing, for-profit enterprise. What he and Page do with their earnings is a decision they alone must negotiate with God. But being invested with their own money in this venture keeps their business instincts keen, their work ethic vigorous, and their spreadsheets scrutinized.

It seems the greater the level of personal investment, the higher the degree of self-interest. That's why investing in for-profit business ventures commands more attention than does making donations to nonprofit organizations. Donors may have a great deal of interest in a cause or mission that they are contributing to, but seldom do they require detailed financial statements or thorough ministry reports. On occasion, nonprofit board members may ask for such details in their role as responsible trustees. But neither trustees nor donors receive a return on their contributions. They expect some level of accountability and some assurance that the program is delivering as promised, but once they've written their check and taken their tax deduction, they rely largely on faith in the organization's leader.

A business investment, on the other hand, is quite different. An investor expects a return. Timely, detailed financial reports are essential. The burn rate of investment capital must be closely monitored. If any of the assumptions made in the business plan prove faulty, decisive corrective action is required. No passive participation here. If the stars line up and the gamble proves right, the investor(s) stands to make attractive earnings. Thus self-interest is high among for-profit investors.

If we intend to move the poverty needle here and in underdeveloped countries, we must increase our level of self-interest. Mission trips, teaching seminars, and service projects will not get the job done. Even economic assistance—microloans, infrastructure improvements, well-digging projects—as important as they may be, do not create wealth. Only profitable businesses do that.

And in the poorest countries, no sizable middle managerial class exists. At the bottom of the economy are microbusinesses that allow people to survive but not thrive, and at the top there is a narrow band of affluent, politically connected families who own and control the country's wealth. In these countries, there is a gaping void called the "missing middle" that prevents both trickle-down and bottom-up development. In order to stimulate the growth of the essential "missing middle," small and midsize for-profit businesses must be created. And that's what we Americans do best.

How to Thrive, Not Just Survive

YOU'LL NEVER MEET A group of five more committed, compassionate volunteer women in any church in the land. They have been on dozens of mission trips, formed personal relationships with poverty-stricken peasants in a remote Nicaraguan village, and started a sewing microenterprise to help village women earn money to support their families, hiring a part-time local Nicaraguan woman to oversee the operation. But after four years of lugging suitcases full of embroidered dishtowels, using their spare bedrooms as warehouses, selling hand-sewn items to every family member, friend, and mission-minded customer they could interest, they were worn out.

Having read *Toxic Charity*, they decided to ask for my counsel. "Is there a way to hand this business off to some other group that will run with it?" they asked. The relationships they had forged with the peasant women were important to them; they were clear about that. They were not looking for a way to disengage personally. They just needed to get the weight of carrying the sewing business off their shoulders.

I understood their dilemma. The board of our Operation Nicaragua ministry was engaged in a similar discussion. After eight years of attempting to market pottery, wooden bowls, hammocks, purses, woven baskets, Christmas ornaments, aluminum crosses made from melted-down Coke cans, and dozens of other artisan creations, our craft business was far from self-sustaining. We had trademarked a brand name (Ojala), set up a website, made inroads with Nicaraguan shops catering to the tourist trade, even ventured into the U.S. market at the Atlanta Merchandise Mart, where national retail chains place large orders.

But there were problems. Only a few of the products had appeal to the tourist market. Fewer still to the market here in the United States. And then there were the challenges of filling larger orders in a timely manner while maintaining acceptable quality standards. It's hard to deliver big quantities when artisans are scattered in different locations doing piecework out of their thatch-roof homes. But we had tried diligently to make it work—for eight years.

We had conducted market research to determine the tastes of tourist and U.S. domestic consumers. We had narrowed the product line to the items most in demand. We had organized artisans into guilds so that best practices could be shared. We had joined forces with international craft distributors. But for all our efforts, it was becoming increasingly clear that the cottage-craft approach was not progressing into a sustainable (let alone profitable) operation.

It had been our sincere hope that we could connect the considerable talents of peasant artisans to markets that would turn their microenterprises into profit-generating businesses. Nicaraguans survive on such little microbusinesses: everyone hustles to earn a few *córdobas* a day. They survive, but they do not thrive. What were we doing wrong?

Even though we were trying to create a business for the ministry (as were the five women who asked me for advice), we were not really approaching the situation *as a business*. If we approached the problem as businesspeople, we would need to bring these enterprises to scale. That would mean enlarging work space, hiring workers, mechanizing production, increasing output, connecting to international markets—in other words, entering the for-profit world of legitimate business. For the average artisan, this is a foreign and intimidating world.

So how do five committed volunteer women from a wealthy U.S. church convert a sewing operation into a self-sustaining business that supports their Nicaraguan friends? How does Ojala enable peasant artisans to prosper? Well, for one thing, we were asking the wrong people these questions. We had been asking our *ministry*-minded friends for their ideas, not *business*-minded people. We had been asking our wealth creators to *donate* to our charity-driven enterprises, not *invest* in them.

What would happen if we saw these experienced business-people as investors instead of donors? They would ask the hard questions—questions about business plans, management experience, marketing research, production capabilities, burn rate, return on investment. The investor's eye invariably goes to the bottom line. But then, if our goal is to alleviate poverty, does it not make sense to invite into the mission those who are gifted in wealth creation?

Successful businesspeople understand job creation. They know that good jobs depend on stable businesses that turn good profits. But if we ask for their help, they are likely to point out the inefficiencies of our cottage-industry approach. They are likely to mention scale and assembly-line efficien-cies. They will explain that a successful manufacturing op-eration must have sufficient capital, experienced leadership, an adequate facility, proficient production processes, effective inventory management, and meticulous quality control. They will probably advise us that without aggressive marketing and unrelenting research and development, a business cannot long survive.

That's the very reason we don't ask them! They compli-cate things. They don't understand that peasant women would rather work in their homes where they can watch their chil-dren and adapt their work schedule around household duties. Businesspeople don't see the value of slower-paced communal village life. They are always pushing to get things done faster, more efficiently, more cost-effectively. They would think nothing of introducing Western business practices into an indigenous culture that has survived for many generations. Yes, there are reasons why we don't ask business types to invest in the mission.

So what are the five committed women to do with their sewing operation? And does Ojala have any future as an economic engine to move peasants out of poverty? Compassion fatigue has brought us to the moment of truth. Are these efforts really about poverty alleviation? Or are they primarily about community building? Both goals are legitimate, I suppose. But when prosperous Americans have the capacity and connections to create businesses that lift people out of a life of grinding poverty, I find it difficult to understand how we can be satisfied doing "relational" ministry built on an artificial economy that offers no way for the poor to rise above survival.

My hope is to discover ways to accomplish both—affirm respect for the indigenous culture while building a profitable business. But it will doubtless be more balanced if *both* "relational" community developers and business-driven entrepreneurs are teamed together. (Traditional missionaries historically have a poor record of economic development.) A well-conceived company can foster a sense of community among its workers. It can offer on-site day care for infants and preschoolers. It can provide health care for employees and families. It can develop skills and leadership that increase employee marketability. It can establish methods of profit sharing that in time can lead to shared ownership. It can stimulate the creation of ancillary businesses such as jitney services and lunch stands. It can inspire dreams for a brighter future. In short, a well-designed business can move a culture from surviving to thriving.

It is difficult to predict what opportunities entrepreneurs from our churches might uncover if we invited them to go with us on mission trips. (Let's call them investment trips.) But the first step is for us to recognize that our wealth producers are not simply funders but are people uniquely gifted with entrepreneurial talents essential to God's plan for flourishing societies, for shalom. They are needed in mission work every bit as much as we need doctors and teachers and, yes, evangelists. In fact, they *are* evangelists; they are the bearers of good news.

Evan Keller, founder of Creating Jobs, demonstrates this by pairing up budding small-business owners in poverty settings with successful American business owners. He has discovered that such mentoring significantly accelerates growth and profitability. Keller prefers mentoring relationships over the "business as mission" approach. "I'm partial to building up the business acumen of people already making a difference in their own communities," he explained to me. "Intellectual capital transfer, in a long-term relational context, can have an amazing impact, but only with the right people." The right people, he stated, are those with standard entrepreneurial personality traits, demonstrated business acumen through the creation of a business with five or more employees, and a teachable temperament that embraces change.

If the visions of five committed volunteer women and the Ojala staff are ever to see their efforts bear the fruit of prosperity, wealth producers must be invited into the process with more than their donations. Whether as mentors or business creators, entrepreneurs are essential to a successful mission. The results will be worth the hassle.

Inviting Wealth Creators in as Partners

So, HOW WILL WE move the poverty needle? Profitable business creation. No people on the face of the earth do this better than Americans. Our pews are packed full of highly skilled, well-honed business experts who have created and run successful, profit-making companies. *These* are the people equipped to take on this challenge. They are the ones who have the instincts, the savvy, the practical know-how to make a business profitable. They understand risk-reward ratios. They know how to construct budgets and project burn rates. They can assess markets and calculate margins. They can estimate workloads and develop timetables. Their skill sets are precisely suited for the task of poverty eradication.

Then why are so few of these business leaders engaged in mission work? No one has asked them—that's why. We have asked them to serve as church officers, head up stewardship committees, run capital campaigns, and fund mission trips, but we have not asked them to use their best talents to move the needle. No one has asked them to create wealth *with* the poor.

If we are serious about moving the poverty needle, we need to put forth a mission call for MBAs rather than MDivs. Those in our pews with expertise in creating successful, profitable enterprises are uniquely qualified to create life-giving jobs in underdeveloped lands. These entrepreneurial members to whom God has entrusted the ability to create wealth are seldom asked to use their best gifts in direct ministry. We ask them to fund our service projects and mission trips, but we rarely ask them to use their business ability in mission. Yet in fact they are the *only* ones equipped to ignite a self-sustaining economy that would enable a community or region to thrive. It's time to change the paradigm.

CHAPTER THREE

Social Entrepreneurs

IN HIS BOOK *How to Change the World*, David Bornstein describes "an emerging landscape of innovators advancing solutions that have the potential to transform life around the globe." He calls these innovators *social entrepreneurs.* The quiet global movement they have initiated he calls *social enterprise.*

Social entrepreneurship is the pursuit of innovative solutions to social problems. Social entrepreneurs are driven to find sustainable solutions to the world's perplexing social problems. They pursue this mission with passion, thinking outside the box, taking risks, not limiting themselves to resources presently in hand. They are outcome-oriented. They draw upon the best thinking in both the business and non-profit worlds and create whatever organizational structures are needed to accomplish their mission: religious and secular, nonprofit and for-profit, and hybrids of various sorts.

Take global businessman and industrialist John Coors, for example.

Many years ago John was on a late-night flight from Amsterdam to Nairobi when he was suddenly awakened from his slumber. According to the flight monitor, the plane was just crossing over the Sahara Desert into sub-Saharan Africa. As John glanced out his window, he saw nothing but a sea of blackness below. For hours, as the plane flew over the desert vastness, he saw not a single light from a village or road. There were millions of people living down there, John was sure. But these people were living in total darkness. That realization struck John with a force he was unable to shake.

John was no stranger to energy needs. Through his previous involvement in the solar power industry, he had learned that one-third of the world has no access to electricity. But of all the dark places on earth, John thought as he peered down from the night sky, sub-Saharan Africa must be the darkest of all. The disturbance he felt in his spirit did not leave when he touched down in Nairobi. Over the following weeks and months, he researched the darkness. His suspicions were confirmed. He discovered that two-thirds of the people living in sub-Saharan Africa had no access to electricity, that five to six hundred million of them still cooked over wood fires. Deforestation was a major problem, as were respiratory ailments due to the inhalation of smoke. The development of clean, affordable sources of light and heat could address a whole spectrum of serious environmental, health, and social issues.

Help Versus Investment

JOHN WAS (AND IS) a visionary. And he had significant capacity. Former leader of America's largest brewing operation and current president and chairman of the highly successful CoorsTek, he had both the resources and the connections to initiate a large-scale energy project. But this venture would be markedly different from any other business enterprise he had undertaken. This one was a calling. To John, it seemed clearly to be a vision authored of God. It would be nonprofit: every dollar of capital invested would go directly to benefit the people it was designed to serve. He would call it Circle of Light.

The concept was technologically simple. The program would set up "energy stores" in rural communities. Operating as member-funded co-ops, these energy stores would provide to each subscribing household a home cooking system—a two-burner stove with propane tank—and a complete home lighting system powered by a twelve-volt battery. The nominal fees charged for exchanging propane tanks and recharging batteries would cover store operations and enable the co-op to be self-sustaining. A minimum of 250 member households, approximately two thousand residents, would be required to initiate a community "energy center." Local co-op boards comprised of community, church, and business leaders (both men and women) would be formed to assume management responsibility and accountability. Circle of Light could thus provide a low-cost, technically simple, sustainable source of modern energy to millions of poor families throughout sub-Saharan Africa and beyond.

The plan was met with enthusiasm, from remote village to national statehouse. Within months, it was providing affordable heat and light to more than one hundred thousand homes in two hundred communities. And there was no end in sight. Circle of Light, it appeared, could actually bring light to an entire darkened world.

But then a problem developed. Even though the cost of the propane refills was modest (given the large-scale purchasing power of the program) and the battery-recharging cost minimal, rural co-op members barely surviving off the land slowly gravitated back to stick-gathering as the most economical source of cooking fuel. And nighttime lighting, though convenient, was something they had done without their whole lives. There were higher priorities for their meager incomes than refilling propane tanks and recharging batteries. Thus, without the steady income stream needed to sustain the energy stores, Circle of Light began to flicker. The government leaders who had been so encouraging had neither the interest nor the resources to underwrite the program. It eventually became apparent to John that the only way to maintain this nonprofit enterprise was to permanently subsidize it with charitable dollars.

And that was something he had no appetite for. Investing in a self-sustaining nonprofit mission was one thing, but indefinitely propping up a program violated certain deeply held values. Reluctantly, John decided to cut his losses: he pulled the plug on Circle of Light.

During a recent Q&A with a group of Florida business leaders, John explained the main lesson he took away from the investment. "I will never again invest a dime—a penny—in a nonprofit that claims to be doing economic development." His tone contained no bitterness; he was merely conveying his realization that a charitable service model, no matter how worthy or how needed its contribution, does not have the capacity to lift the poor out of their poverty. "The poor need jobs!" John declared. The reality is that without for-profit, wealth-generating businesses, the poor will remain at a subsistence level, scratching out an existence, their hopes and dreams shackled to the daily pressures of survival. Without employment that offers a brighter future, they will predictably resign themselves to smoky cooking fires and nature's cycles of darkness and light.

Did John give up on helping the poor? No, instead he focused on what *would* bring the results he was looking for—actually moving people out of poverty—and on learning from his nonprofit mistakes. It was the realization described above, John said, that impelled him to initiate a values-based private investment fund to stimulate business growth in sub-Saharan Africa. It is called One Thousand & One Voices (1K1V). "Capitalism and business done well—not socialism or philanthropy—is the only proven path for economic development to lift multitudes from poverty. People in Africa are yearning for jobs. Only business can create an expanding jobs base, but business can succeed only if it has investment, and investment will come only if the returns warrant the risk. I believe today they do, and that is why my family has become involved in the One Thousand & One Voices movement."

John has set about raising $300 million from wealthy families in the United States and Africa to invest in promising African businesses, thus enabling them to grow and multiply at a faster rate and create increasing numbers of well-paying jobs. His five-year vision is to raise $5 billion from five hundred families to invest in great businesses all over the world in impoverished countries. "The foundation of this movement is the realization that we don't need more philanthropy; we don't need more aid in Africa," John said. "We need more investment because we need to create jobs."

Contrary to popular perception, the economy of sub-Saharan Africa has a promising rate of growth—greater than European markets. But in order for developing-market businesses to flourish, they need "patient" financial capital, which traditional private equity funds are reluctant to provide. Each family investing with John in the 1K1V fund makes a three-dimensional commitment: relational capital that leverages family connections and reputation, intellectual capital that leverages their business and industry knowledge, and patient financial capital that provides the longer-term funding that developing-market businesses need to grow.

John Coors's journey into the darkness of the world's most impoverished people began with a divine awakening at thirty-seven thousand feet. His *heart* drew him toward addressing some of the most obvious needs of isolated, underserved populations. But it was not until his *mind* became fully engaged, not until he came face-to-face with the fundamentals of moving the poverty needle, that he landed on a bedrock remedy. "The pathway to economic freedom—real prosperity for millions living in poverty—is through values-based private investment grounded in the time-tested principles of free enterprise." And he is not the only one who believes this. A new, visionary movement is stirring—one that embodies enormous hope for the poor.

The blessing of wealth is meant for the shalom of the entire community, not to be hoarded for personal gain. Managed well, wealth provides a stable lifestyle for a workforce and their families, stimulates ancillary enterprises, and contributes to the prosperity of the whole village or region.

The Mission of Business

IT IS TIME WE brought theological balance to our understanding of wealth. With the entire world awakening to the reality that healthy economic systems are fundamental to the elimination of extreme poverty, perhaps this is a moment for resourced members of the Western church—who have an unparalleled capacity to create profitable businesses—to step forward. This is the time when the church can begin to see itself as more than just a purveyor of compassionate service, but also as a catalyst of just and fruitful economies. My hope is that this movement will become a turning point: that the wealthiest church in history will awaken to the reality that its job is not just saving souls, but also bringing economic wholeness to struggling souls too long resigned to unending poverty.

The existing physical and human assets overlooked in depressed regions often must be capitalized in order to create wealth if the poor are to thrive. This can take a multitude of forms: agribusiness, tourism, manufacturing, or a host of other possibilities. But in order for this to happen, businesspeople with vision and access to capital must be invited in—and must accept the challenge. These new missionaries of social entrepreneurship must be capable people who have come to the realization that their deal-making instincts, their penchant for turning a profit, are gifts of God to enable them to do well and do good at the same time.

John Coors is just one example, and he is just beginning his new venture. He is by no means alone in this effort to blend mission and business. A new kind of missionary is on the rise. A quarter century ago there were very few nongovernmental organizations (NGOs) outside the United States concerned with development work. Now there are many thousands of them all over the globe. Ashoka, the largest and most recognized international network of social entrepreneurs, supports more than two thousand social enterprises in seventy different countries.

The visions that drive social entrepreneurs are inspiring, sometimes even grandiose. Some of these entrepreneurs, driven to fulfill their visions, have changed the course of modern history. Muhammad Yunus, founder of the Grameen Bank, certainly has. His successful microlending experiment among the poorest classes of India proved to the banking world that working with the poor is both good business and profitable business. His microlending model has now gone mainstream, resulting in billions of dollars of small-business loans becoming available to the world's most undercapitalized microentrepreneurs. In spite of the unfortunate recent trend of many microloans becoming misused as consumer debt rather than small-business loans, the availability of capital is essential for the poor to emerge from poverty.

Yunus's history-altering example may be the exception, in terms of breadth. Most social enterprises are more limited in scale and scope. But that is one reason why the field churns with such energy and excitement. It is an open, uncharted new frontier that beckons to adventuresome visionaries.

Another example of a vision exceptionally executed is found in four college friends from the Wharton School of Business in Philadelphia who devised a way to market prescription eyewear online at well below the normal cost while offering improved vision to the poor, who often have no access to eyeglasses. The creative and adventuresome foursome of Neil Blumenthal, Andrew Hunt, Jeffrey Raider, and David Gilboa took on the eyewear monopoly that had set the elevated pricing for prescription eyeglasses. Together, they founded Warby Parker "with a rebellious spirit and a lofty objective: to create designer eyewear at revolutionary prices while leading the way for socially conscious businesses" (Warbyparker.com). By circumventing traditional retail stores and going directly to customers through their website, Warby Parker provides high-quality, fashionable prescription eyewear at a fraction of the price. And it's working. So is their strategy for giving sight to the vision-impaired poor of the world. "We believe that everyone has the right to see," they boldly declare. They aspire to impact a global population of nearly one billion who are deprived of achieving full potential because of poor eyesight. To date they have distributed more than a million pairs of glasses through their buy-one-give-one marketing strategy.

But theirs is no soft-hearted charity approach. Neil Blumenthal understands the dangers of unhealthy dependency. VisionSpring, a nonprofit he directed for five years, gave glasses away, but then discovered the economic and social benefits of equipping microentrepreneurs in poor communities to operate low-cost eyeglass franchises. Warby Parker now employs that VisionSpring model, which imparts not only sight to the visually impaired, but economic vitality as well.

Patrick Woodyard is another young entrepreneur with a mission. He started an innovative for-profit shoe business that is gaining momentum. While his Nisolo brand is similar to TOMS (a company that has given away thirty-five million pairs of shoes worldwide through its buy-one-give-one approach), Patrick's methodology is strikingly different. He saw the grinding poverty in Peru, but he saw something else too—the talent of local craftspeople to design and create shoes from old tires and scrap leather. Instead of adopting a giveaway strategy à la TOMS, Patrick decided to build on the capacities of local artisans. His Nisolo line features fine, handcrafted shoes that are marketed internationally with the motto "Wear change." The goal, according to the company's website, is to empower talented artisans in the developing world, allowing them to shape their future by way of their extraordinary work. Patrick is convinced that giving shoes away does not achieve his own goal of addressing the root causes of poverty. Prior to launching his Nisolo enterprise, he did his due diligence in order to better shape his business's strategies. He discovered that even the poorest villages seemed to have an ample supply of shoes available. Millions of used shoes find their way into the most desolate places—some given away by nonprofits, some sold on the local market. Based on his research, he felt that the TOMS shoe-drops were awkward, feel-good publicity events that had no lasting economic benefit. Worse, giveaway programs can even undercut small entrepreneurs trying to make a living on local production. Used clothing imports, for instance, caused a

50 percent increase in unemployment in the African textile industry from 1981 to 2000. And between 1992 and 2006, a half million workers in Nigeria lost their jobs due to the inflow of donated clothing. Patrick's research convinced him that jobs, not donations, were what the poor needed.

While Patrick does invest 10 percent of his profits to provide educational opportunities for local children, he believes that employment, not charity, is the most effective way to enable the poor to emerge from poverty. To date, his Nisolo strategy has generated hundreds of small, profitable businesses that have, in turn, spawned thousands of decent-paying jobs.

Social enterprise would seem on the surface to have a more redemptive purpose than typical business ventures. But I'm not so sure. Ethical businesses make a significant contribution to their industry and to society (regardless of their product). They are the primary source of wealth that stimulates local economies, that in turn creates jobs, generates tax revenue, and produces beneficial (and competitive) goods and services. "Ethical" is the operative word. Fortunately, businesses are becoming increasingly sensitive to environmental and social concerns, a sensitivity heightened no doubt by watchdog advocacy groups. The corporate world is discovering that it is good business to be not only profitable, but socially and environmentally friendly as well. But a myopic focus on profit and gain when we evaluate businesses can make us blind to all the social good that businesses make possible—a result that even businesses themselves can miss.

Recently, a new type of corporate structure has appeared on the scene to encourage ethical business behavior. It's called the "for-benefit" organization, or "B corp." This structure offers a middle ground between for-profit and nonprofit organizations. It challenges the traditional dichotomy—that nonprofits do good and for-profits make money—by offering a legal means to accomplish both. The goal of the "B corp" company is to create products and services that benefit the economic, social, and environmental arenas simultaneously. Legal classification for the for-benefit corporation is currently being created by some states, which directs how profitability is to be shared among these three bottom-line beneficiaries.

So does all this socially conscious entrepreneurial activity signal a new era of enlightenment and compassion? Renowned economist Jeffrey Sachs is hopeful. He has been monitoring global poverty for years and is encouraged by recent trends. In 2001 there were 1.1 billion people living on less than two dollars a day. This is extreme poverty. Sachs believes that, with dedicated action, extreme poverty could be eliminated by 2025. And he is not alone in his thinking. All 191 members of the United Nations committed to this objective in the 2002 UN Millennium Development Goals. By 2005, when Sachs released *The End of Poverty*, that goal was more than halfway met. And the trend continues. He is convinced that Millennium Development investments to improve infrastructure (roads, bridges, transportation, electricity) and strengthen responsible government create the conditions for businesses to flourish and economies to grow. Once a country has reached the first rung of economic development, it is on its way to eliminating extreme poverty. A culture that encourages businesses, not more externally funded charitable services, is the key to ending poverty. The historic growth in economic development that we are currently experiencing, according to Jeffrey Sachs, is widespread and real.

But economists like Sachs view reality from a sanitary thirty-thousand-foot distance, not at a grassroots level where social entrepreneurs sweat over spreadsheets. The amazing gains in global poverty alleviation are primarily the result of mushroom explosions in the economies of India and China. Very little change has taken place in sub-Saharan Africa or Latin America. Nevertheless, the macro principle holds true at the micro level: economic growth, not humanitarian aid or NGO proliferation, is clearly the largest factor in eliminating poverty.

So what role do entrepreneurs play in this epic drama? They are the dreamers, the risk-takers, the ones close enough to the earth to test ideas, problem-solve, then try again. They are the heart and soul of any flourishing economy. The small and medium businesses they create provide the lion's share of good jobs. And when their business instincts are coupled with a social conscience, everyone prospers. They can be found in every land, though conditions must be conducive if they are to thrive.

For some reason, in the providence of God, America has been blessed with an abundance of ambitious, adventuresome, business-minded risk-takers who have propelled our nation to the forefront of economic prosperity. They account for 80 percent of our new jobs annually. Their small and medium enterprises produce 50 percent of the nation's GNP. The pews of our churches are filled with these ethical and generous dreamers and risk-takers. They fund our service projects and mission trips. Some even participate personally in business training seminars for aspiring entrepreneurs in the inner city and in underdeveloped countries. Billionaire Robert Kern, for instance, recently allocated a large portion of his estate to educating ministers in the fundamentals of how the economy works.

The church is also getting into the act. Millions of volunteers fan out across the globe each year to serve the world's poor. Religious tourism is big business. Very big business. In North America, where fifty thousand U.S. churches have religious travel programs—mission trips, pilgrimages, visits to holy sites, retreats and monastery stays, and religious cruises—ministry tourism generates more than $10 billion a year. Short-term mission trips account for approximately one-third of those dollars. This compassionate force embodies powerful economic potential. But unlike most other types of tourism, mission trips contribute very little to local economies. One reason is that mission-trippers come to serve, not consume. They spend their money on airfare and projects rather than on merchandise and excursions.

As I discussed in *Toxic Charity*, at first glance mission

trips would appear to be self-sacrificial efforts bringing much-needed assistance to the struggling poor. A closer look, however, reveals a different picture. The poor need to earn income. Microbusiness is the way most families survive in underdeveloped countries. Selling fruit and vegetables at roadside stands, handcrafting pottery and wood carvings to market at tourist stops, sewing embroidered dresses made on treadle sewing machines—these are the types of small enterprises that keep the poor alive. Some of their products are bartered or sold to neighbors. The higher profits, however, come from tourists. Families with enviable locations near busy tourist stops do best, at least during tourist season. Tourists mean sales, and sales put bread on the table. The groan of a diesel tour bus can be a heavenly sound, signaling the arrival of new customers.

But not all arriving tourists evoke such positive responses. The sight of a van loaded with T-shirted mission-trippers elicits the opposite reaction. The short-term missionaries on board are unwitting saboteurs of the fragile micromerchant economy. Instead of bolstering local enterprise through their purchases, these tourists-on-a-mission eviscerate local businesses by flooding the market with suitcases full of free clothes, shoes, and other saleable goods. Their naive kindness undercuts the very system locals depend on for their livelihood—as Patrick Woodyard confirmed before he launched his Nisolo brand.

By asking more of the people we serve than to simply accept our handouts, we can become a stimulus to a life-giving economic system. First of all, let's agree that religious tourism is legitimate business, a substantial industry that can undergird an entire national economy. Look at Rome or Israel, for instance. Of course, short-term missionaries are more than mere tourists: we come with a redemptive purpose. And that redemptive purpose could and should include more than temporary aid. It should have a sustainable effect on the alleviation of poverty.

With just a modicum of creativity, we could enhance the self-sufficiency (not to speak of the dignity) of our local hosts by fostering new enterprises. A starting place would be simply to become the paying clientele of indigenous providers of lodging, food, local transportation, and other hosting functions. In other words, create a market for new microenterprises in hospitality. That market could be either church-based or community-based. It could employ local talent in the culinary arts, modest lodging (perhaps in a church), even entertainment. A legitimate exchange rate based on local economic realities could be negotiated—one that is neither exploitive nor extravagant. Instead of our being an imposition on pastors and mission leaders that pulls them away from their ministry duties to create make-work to make us feel useful, we become paying customers who strengthen local capacity. In this way we become life-giving clients for new microentrepreneurs whom we have enabled to enter the religious tourism business. It's a place to start.

Using Social Enterprise to Become Better Missionaries

OF COURSE, IF WE really wanted to maximize our impact on the lives of the poor, we could convert our mission trips into business-as-ministry ventures. Instead of inviting any old tenderhearted volunteer to sign up, we could become much more selective in our mission strategy. We could offer to the poor our most valued talent: business acumen. Would it not be an act of redemptive love to share this resource with struggling people who have a strong work ethic and an abundance of unexploited resources but who lack training, capital, and access to markets? Indeed, we could have major, lasting impact on the poor if we challenged our business-minded volunteers to create or enhance wealth-generating enterprises in underdeveloped communities. Making money *with* the poor, after all, is the highest form of charity.

Here's an idea. Instead of planning another mission trip with service-minded volunteers, how about putting together an "investment trip" with a group of business leaders? Spend a week exploring unexploited business opportunities in the region where the church has been involved. Entrepreneurs will see things that servers miss—bamboo growing wild along the road, tilapia that thrive in the local lakes, the demand for an adequate ferry service. Who knows what ideas might be stimulated by curious and inventive minds!

One good idea and one seasoned entrepreneur is all it takes to ignite a business. A midlife half-timer from the church (or other group) ready to move on to his next venture may be primed to take on the challenge . . . or a younger, energetic entrepreneur who is ready for a mission. The church can begin searching and praying for the "economic missionary" God has prepared for this task. Getting investors to back a well-conceived business venture, especially when it has both a redemptive purpose and a reasonable rate of return, is not such a difficult challenge for a committed group of successful businesspeople.

Take the Phoenix Community of Atlanta, for example. This young, mission-minded church was transformed by their visits to Central America. After witnessing the poverty, they pledged to become a giving church, spending as little as possible on themselves and investing largely in the lives of those in need. Rather than build a church building, they decided to worship in a rented warehouse that could double as a church-run nonprofit business. Their social enterprise? Phoenix Community Coffee, a business with a triple bottom line: income for their church, for other churches, and for peasant farmers. The four members of their pastoral team now spend half their time pastoring and the other half working in the coffee business. Being "working" pastors gives them credibility with their "working" congregation, they claim.

The church has established personal relationships with coffee growers in Guatemala and Panama and imports tons of green coffee beans, which they roast in their warehouse before packaging and shipping to 250 partners around the country. "Great coffee, great cause" is their marketing motto. They offer their partners wholesale prices on high-grade coffee that partners (mostly churches and religious groups) then sell to raise funds for their missions and projects. The direct relationship with growers avoids brokers and pays growers well above commodity prices for their beans. Phoenix Community Coffee generates income to support their local church budget, helps other church groups raise money for missions, and enables Central American farmers to prosper.

Rob Smith is another example of a businessman who is combining his faith and his business acumen. A successful boat manufacturer in Seattle, Rob observed on a visit to Africa an obsolete ferry system barely functioning on Lake Victoria. He immediately saw the need and potential for a modern ferry network connecting the growing cities around the massive lake. Poorly maintained roads around the lake, jammed with passenger buses and diesel trucks, slowed travel and commerce between cities to a snail's pace. Rob's imagination was stirred. He could envision a fast passenger ferry system that could grow into a freight service and even a railroad transportation connector. He was captivated. Conversations with government leaders confirmed his assessment. The following months were consumed in due diligence, consultation with professionals in the commercial ferry industry, and painstaking calculations to construct a bankable business plan. And finally a launch: EarthWise Ferries sailed its first craft into Lake Victoria loaded with excited passengers.

EarthWise is more than a for-profit company. It has a transformative mission. Businesspeople, local residents, and tourists are now able to cross the lake to conduct business. Commuting times have been cut drastically (versus traveling around the lake by road). Tickets are competitively priced. And that's not all. A functioning infrastructure means lower costs of goods to the poor. The company itself has the potential to generate hundreds of direct jobs, besides facilitating new business start-ups as lower freight costs allow new competitiveness. EarthWise ferries burn pure vegetable oil, which provides a source of income for potentially hundreds of local farmers.

The vision of one entrepreneur can have a substantial impact on the poverty needle. Is it not time to intentionally engage the business-gifted saints in the mission?

CHAPTER FOUR

Return on Investment

ONE WOULD THINK THAT THE tons of food, mountains of clothing, incalculable hours of service, and billions of dollars that are given each year to assist the poor would move the poverty needle. They do not. Advocates contend, however, that poverty would be far worse were it not for these charitable donations. Perhaps. Heartwarming stories continue to abound—the homeless family supported until they got back on their feet; a miracle coincidence of food appearing at exactly the right moment; a life forever changed by the kindhearted act of a stranger. Such accounts are inspiring and motivating. But anecdotal. Get a little distance from the emotion, take an objective look at the larger reality, and it becomes disturbingly obvious that the poor are only getting poorer.

Let's be honest. Helping the poor to become self-sufficient, though certainly a desired outcome, is generally not our only (or even primary) motivation for giving. Charity is good for *us*. It is, after all, the mark of good citizenship. Charity provides volunteer opportunities for nearly every church, synagogue, and mosque in the land. It is a value that parents want to instill in their children. It is even good for business. And because charity is so widely embraced as good—good for our society, good for our souls—it is easy to assume that it is also good for the recipients. It is not. Not the way we have been practicing it.

Very few people in our society are so severely dysfunctional that they have no capacity to give. Even the chronic homeless with mental illness or addiction have something to contribute. Everyone, no matter how impaired or down on their luck, has a talent, a capability, a strength to bring to the table. To overlook these abilities, to offer pity instead of opportunity, is to diminish rather than empower. Subsidizing nonproductivity disempowers the poor. Doing for others what they have the capacity to do for themselves is debilitating. Unfortunately, this describes most of our charity—from donating toys at Christmas to passing out socks to street people to providing free soup and cots at homeless shelters. Without a means of exchange, the recipients of our benevolence remain objects of our pity. As we've already seen, the most effective programs require participants to assume responsibility for their own development. These programs discourage free handouts and other kindhearted subsidies that erode a work ethic and hinder the growth of personal initiative. Which is to say that most of the giveaway volunteer efforts initiated by religious and charitable groups work at cross-purposes with programs committed to moving people out of poverty. Such giveaway programs consider their existence proof of their success; they hardly ever evaluate their success in terms of moving the poverty needle.

In the business world, however, CEOs and CFOs constantly monitor their success rate in relation to their bottom line. How? With three simple words: return on investment. ROI is fairly easy to calculate. Is the investment profitable or not? What is the rate of return? Dollar and cents earnings are objective measures. But calculating the return on *charitable* investments is far more elusive.

Donors do, however, expect to see lasting good accomplished through their gifts. This expectation is mirrored in Andrew Carnegie's stated purpose for his philanthropic investments: to accomplish "real and permanent good in this world" and to create "ladders on which the aspiring can rise." Compassionate givers may pay a utility bill to keep a family's heat turned on, but they certainly don't want this to become a habit. They may provide a bus pass so an unemployed person can get to a job interview, but they expect this to lead to self-sufficiency. Such expectations are not always verbalized, but they are certainly assumed.

So when it comes to charitable giving, what's the rate of return, the return on the time and resources invested in the cause of helping people in need? One way we might measure a charitable ROI is by monitoring self-reliance. For instance, when a young, unskilled mother is hired as a trainee in our community thrift store, she learns to operate the cash register, tally the day's sales, and handle customer service, all while developing good work habits; this training prepares her for a successful entry into the economic mainstream. A positive ROI is realized when she secures full-time employment with a stable company that pays a livable wage.

Another criterion by which to assess charitable ROI is the quality of relationship between giver and recipient. Reciprocal relationships in which both giver and recipient contribute value (bartering, for example) are mutually beneficial. Trust, accountability, and even genuine friendships can grow from interdependent relationships. Take a look at Betty, a neighbor of mine who occasionally requested food from our church's food pantry. The food was for her grandchildren, whom she was raising on her own. When she was invited to assist in the nursery during one of the church's services, she was delighted. Betty loved children, and this soon became apparent to parents whose infants she cared for during church activities. She became a trusted nursery volunteer, eager to serve and greatly appreciated by church members. That healthy relationship is proof of a positive ROI.

Another ROI criterion that church folks often attempt to assess is the spiritual results of their giving. Addressing the temporal needs of the poor is important, but of far greater importance is their eternal salvation. Inserting Bibles or gospel tracts in donated food boxes is one way religious givers address the spiritual dimension. More aggressive groups require attendance at religious services as a precondition for receiving meals or lodging. The return on their investment can be calculated by the number of conversions recorded. Or, better yet, by recipients' ongoing participation in a local community of faith.

There are obviously many other measures for calculating the yield on charitable investments: steady employment, responsible money management, skill development, stable housing, to name just a few. Regardless of the criteria we choose to evaluate, however, one thing soon becomes obvious: significant due diligence is required to obtain reliable data. How do we know that the recipient of our bus pass, for instance, is using it to get to a job interview? How do we know that the woman getting a food box from our church pantry isn't making the rounds to other churches, telling the same hard-luck story? We don't. Not unless we become personally involved over time in a genuine relationship with the people we're serving. And most of us are far too busy for this kind of messy, time-consuming involvement. So what are the alternatives?

One approach is a system of accountability. A computerized distribution network among churches and service providers that tracks goods and services can provide a continuum of services, as well as help prevent abuse. But it is not as simple as investing in a state-of-the-art software system. The city of Myrtle Beach, South Carolina, discovered this when they tried to address their homeless problem. The mayor's office initiated the effort to coordinate the activities of some sixty homeless-serving agencies and churches. Getting all the groups in one room was a significant challenge, but nothing compared to convincing them to work together. A handful of the leading churches and agencies eventually bought in, and a coordinating committee was formed. It consisted of influential pastors, prominent directors of homeless ministries, city officials, downtown business leaders, and foundation executives. Together, committee members put into place a coordinated service delivery plan. A local agency was selected by the committee to provide intake, assess the level of need, issue an ID card, and refer clients to the appropriate church or agency. Screened clients presented their ID card in order to obtain food, clothing, shelter, or other support services. At the same time, the committee approved a general fund that combined public, philanthropic, charitable, church, and business dollars to support participating programs. The result was a citywide effort that produced an accountable continuum of services for the homeless. A system of accountability is certainly one way to help ensure that our charitable dollars are being used responsibly.

Of course, not all those in need choose to participate in any given system—some feel they can do better hustling on their own. And not all churches and ministries elect to join the system; some would rather do their own thing. So the accountability system approach is not without its flaws. It does, however, introduce a measure of responsibility to an otherwise unmonitored charity environment. And when it functions at its best, it provides a continuum of care that is both accountable and comprehensive.

But accountable systems such as described above, though effective in controlling misuse, do little to build community. Like government bureaucracies, they process and expedite, but they have little time for relationship building. Personal relationships happen at the program level where one-on-one time is invested and the tangle of perplexing problems is sorted out. Short-term crisis intervention may be a legitimate first step, but the ministries that yield the best ROI are longer-term, deeper-delving programs—programs that conduct thorough individual assessments, map out personally tailored development plans, and commit to consistent follow-through. These higher-yield programs cannot deliver the high-volume numbers that handout programs do, but their impact is far more lasting.

And the spiritual impact? It is the poor, you may recall, to whom Jesus said his kingdom belongs. "Blessed are you poor, for yours is the kingdom of God" (Luke 6:20). A more affirming starting point might be to inquire about recipients' spiritual journey, with the assumption that each recipient has in all likelihood had some sort of encounter with the Divine.

For those consumed with survival, prayer is a fairly common response. I discovered this when I first moved into an inner city. Many of my neighbors who gathered for meals and programs at our neighborhood church struggled perpetually with life-controlling issues. Prayer to them was like a floating log to someone who is drowning. Their faith somehow helped them to survive through some very dark circumstances. A man I came to know named Zeke is a good example. When I met Zeke, he was sleeping rough, spending most nights under the bushes in the park. He was an alcoholic, destitute, friendless, broken. Once a hard worker, he had become unable to hold a job. One day, while Zeke was helping me patch a leak on the church roof, he said something that threw my theology off balance. "Bob, I ain't no Christian," he said, "but I love my Jesus." Zeke was the polar opposite of my concept of a Christian (though I had to admit that there were similarities with the man in Jesus's story who stood downcast at the back of the temple beating his chest and pleading, "God be merciful to me a sinner"—the one who went away justified). Zeke forced me to ponder whether a broken (and admittedly self-destructive) person could also be a person of faith.

Over the next thirty years, I crossed paths with Zeke periodically. Nothing changed much for him during that time, just an ever-deepening descent into the pathological pit that ensnared him. Recently I saw him on the street hustling money for booze, right eye gouged out, white beard matted, mind nearly gone. He told me that the preacher down at the church wouldn't have much to do with him anymore. "But I still love my Jesus," he affirmed. I couldn't help wondering if it was his faith that had kept him going for decades of harsh street life.

ROI for the Zekes of this world can hardly be judged

as "ladders on which the aspiring can rise." The severely dysfunctional—those with disabilities due to misfortune as well as those with self-inflicted impairments—may never be able to pull their own weight. But *all* people were created with an innate desire to be useful. Identifying recipients' strengths and capacities and employing those in meaningful exchange (as in mopping tar on a church roof), even if such capacities will never lead to self-reliance, affords dignity, which comes only through usefulness. And that may be the optimal ROI for support given to those who cannot become fully self-sufficient.

Activities or Outcomes?

BUT THE MOST READILY measurable return on investment for charitable giving comes down to a simple question—activities or outcomes?

I met some time ago with a pastor of a suburban megachurch. As he and I spoke candidly about the impact of his ministry, I asked him the following: If his church were disbanded tomorrow, would his community even realize it? By the surprised look on his face, it was apparent that in his twenty-five years of ministry, no one had asked that question. His knee-jerk reaction was "Of *course* they would!" He went on to explain that his church had a large presence in the community—nearly twenty acres of well-designed facilities with a sanctuary that accommodated five thousand. And their private Christian school provided a quality education to several hundred students. The church's generous budget included emergency assistance for many families in need, he said. Scores of small groups from the church engaged in service projects in the city as well as mission trips abroad. Yes, his church was about far more than filling the pews on Sunday. Certainly it was having a positive impact on the surrounding community.

So why did the question trouble him so?

If church members were polled, they would certainly have positive things to say about the church's impact, but of course, they were insiders, direct beneficiaries. And besides, they came from all over the metropolitan area—hardly an accurate barometer of the influence of the church on the immediate community. What if a survey were taken of those who lived within a radius of, say, three miles around the church? What would that reveal? And what would the mayor and city council members say, or school principals, or the police? Would there be a public outcry if the church announced on Sunday that it was closing its doors and moving away? Oh, some might worry that this was an early warning sign of decline in the area. And it would definitely capture the attention of the real estate brokers. But would the community view the church's closing as a tragic loss? Would the social fabric be significantly weakened? "In all honesty, probably not," the pastor reluctantly admitted.

It was a sobering admission. Could a flagship church, a model emulated by scores, even hundreds, of churches across the country, a successful example of how to "do church right" in a day of denominational decline—could it be that such a church would be deemed "insignificant" by its community? Even worse, could it be considered a non-taxpaying nuisance, a competitor to the local schools, a traffic problem, an institutional encroachment upon a residential neighborhood? Could it be that church growth was not synonymous with kingdom advancement? Could a church truly love God while at the same time offending its neighbors? These questions were understandably disconcerting to a pastor who had invested the best years of his life building what he believed to be an effective church.

If these questions, or even just some of them, were answered in the affirmative, the pastor realized that corrective action would be necessary. What would have to change for the community to begin to view the church as an asset? That was the primary question—and one he decided to pose to his elder board. Certainly the congregation needed to remain committed to the fundamental mission of the church: seeker-sensitive worship, evangelism outreach, and small-group discipleship had to remain their bedrock. But how could they engage with the community around them in ways that would be welcomed, appreciated, and not perceived to be mere marketing strategies? The discussion led into a rather profound theological question: How can a church both love God and love its neighbor? The answer proved much more complex than merely inviting neighbors to come to church or increasing the congregation's benevolence budget.

One of the benefits of pastoring a megachurch is that the pool of available talent is expansive. In addition to a strong elder board of respected professionals, the church was blessed with an abundance of good minds—creative ones that could dissect an issue, analyze it, research it, and come up with an effective plan of action. A blue-ribbon task force would be formed, the elders agreed, with the mandate to come up with a plan to address the question, How can our church have the most positive impact on our community?

Two years later, I reconnected with the pastor's full-time point man, who had been hired to direct both the task force and any program changes that the group might recommend. A "community engagement strategy" had been researched, thoroughly vetted, distilled into operational format, and adopted by the elders. Though the plan had already been approved and was ready to be rolled out, someone had suggested that it might be prudent to get input from a seasoned veteran who had spent much of his life engaged in hands-on community ministry: me. The lunch meeting might have been perfunctory, but I was honored nonetheless. The young man hired to implement the plan seemed genuinely interested in my counsel. I was immediately impressed with him—a business type with good communication skills and a winsome smile. His excitement was contagious. He showed me a well-designed, easy-to-understand diagram of his strategy—a two-tier approach to involve all ten thousand–plus of their members in community service and racial reconciliation. The plan was brilliant in its simplicity.

First, the church would start no new programs. There were plenty of programs, agencies, schools, and ministries out there in need of committed volunteers. Rather than spending its resources on program start-ups, the church would develop a comprehensive database of worthwhile volunteer opportunities, then promote, organize, and manage the placement of church members in those settings. In that process, hundreds of thousands of service-hours would be invested in the community, addressing a broad range of social as well as spiritual needs. It would be good news for the community and at the same time encourage members to live out a more holistic gospel.

"What's your target area?" I inquired.

"A fifteen-mile radius around the church," the director responded.

This was essentially the size of a major city, I commented. Perhaps it was a bit ambitious, he agreed; on the other hand, their members came from all over the metropolitan area.

"And how will you measure success?" I continued.

"When all ten thousand of our members are actively engaged in service in the community," he said without a hint of hesitation. Somehow I believed that he and his highly motivated task force could pull it off.

"That would be a measure of activities, not outcomes, wouldn't it?" I pressed. "What impact would all this activity actually accomplish? And how would you measure the impact?"

Silence.

The church's strategy was built on the assumption that

increased volunteerism would automatically translate into societal transformation. That assumption certainly had face-validity. Yet how could this theory be tested? With such a massive target area, there would be no way of knowing if a volunteer force of ten thousand disbursed across a population of millions was having any impact at all. Even more disquieting for my young friend, I acquainted him with a growing body of respected research that raises serious doubts about his strategy's underlying assumption. An increase in volunteerism actually tends to *increase* dependency among the served, say researchers. As important as volunteers can be, without wise and experienced leadership and careful monitoring, they can ultimately do more harm than good, regardless of how noble their intentions. This did not come as welcome news.

My young director friend moved hurriedly on to explain the second tier of his program—racial reconciliation. He described a plan to bring his predominantly white church together with a large black church for a joint Easter celebration that would fill the civic center. The two groups would plan the event together, blend their choirs, share the pulpit, and worship God in visible unity. The event would require an extraordinary amount of planning, joint committee work, and logistical coordinating. But it would be worth the effort, everyone agreed. It would be an inspiring demonstration of the unity of a diverse family of faith, an Easter long to be remembered.

"And then what?" I asked. It came out a little more bluntly than I had intended, but I couldn't help wondering where reconciliation would go from there, from that single event. Black and white Christians working together, getting to know each other better, and worshipping God together would be a wonderful first step. And a combined Easter service could certainly be soul-stirring. But when the event was over, would the congregations continue to build on the relationships that had been formed, or would they simply return to their separate communities and segregated circles? Was there a plan to take reconciliation to the next level?

Again, silence.

"May I suggest an idea for next steps?" My young friend nodded—not a very convincing nod, but enough to give me license to continue. Buy some land together, I said, located somewhere between your two churches, enough for a decent-size subdivision. Pull your real estate professionals together and design an attractive residential neighborhood. Market it to both your memberships. Invite families from both congregations to buy into the dream of a reconciled community—a beloved community, if you will. Raise your children together. Share your lives together as neighbors. Celebrate those who take the risk as true reconcilers, the ones modeling through their daily lives what the gospel of reconciliation is all about. I could feel myself getting excited; the ideas were flowing. In my initial enthusiasm, I ignored my lunch partner's frequent glances at his watch, but when he started gathering up his papers I began to suspect that this "reconciled neighbors" vision wasn't resonating with him. He had been hoping for an endorsement, not a critique, and certainly not a major modification. He already had his plan. Big numbers were what he needed—ten thousand volunteers, a civic center full of worshippers. He motioned to the waitress for our check and slipped his materials into his briefcase. With a warm smile and a handshake, we parted.

Differentiating Between Activities and Outcomes

ACTIVITIES OR OUTCOMES—HOW CAN you tell which is which? It's a fair question that is gaining some traction among funders these days. Take, for example, the proposal I developed to secure funding for a community development project FCS was initiating in the long-neglected neighborhood called South Atlanta. A foundation responded positively to our submitted proposal. It was considering a very substantial grant to support our transformation effort. But first the foundation board, mostly businesspeople, wanted an answer to a very businesslike question: How will we know that our investment has produced tangible, positive results? It was a reasonable question—no, more than reasonable, it was a *responsible* question. And it's a question that comes up a lot. How can you measure transformation in a community?

The Community Design Center, a research group out of Georgia Tech, had studied the issue and were engaged to conduct a longitudinal study for us. The first step was to define the target area; then establish baseline data on an index of seven measurable indicators of community health—home ownership, education levels, crime statistics, religious involvement, and so forth; and then track changes in those indicators over a five-year period and plot the direction of movement. If the trend is upward, toward health, then it's reasonable to assume that the plan being assessed is working. If the data remains static or declines, we can assume that the program is not having the intended impact. The results would not be highly scientific, but they would be reasonably reliable indicators. The foundation agreed to add the additional cost of this third-party research to their grant.

The measurement of outcomes does several things, I discovered. It forces benefactors to concentrate their efforts toward specific goals rather than take a generalized, serve-the-neighborhood approach. For example, if reducing drug trafficking in the community were one of the objectives, then a targeted strategy would have to be implemented to, say, eliminate crack houses, establish neighborhood watches, focus police attention on drug-traffic corners, and create wholesome alternatives for youth. Or, if housing were an issue, slumlords would have to be confronted, code enforcement beefed up, homeowner training initiated, rehab and new construction funded. Such goal-oriented activities, if effective, always translate into measurable results.

Another benefit of measuring outcomes is accountability. Those who invest valuable resources—whether time, expertise, or dollars—have a right to know if their investments are actually accomplishing anything of lasting value. A church that provides money and volunteers to build a house for a needy family can see the tangible results of their efforts: a family moving into a new home. But they also have a right to know that the family will maintain their new home, that there is a plan in place to improve the surrounding neighborhood. Otherwise, the charming house could deteriorate, drug dealers might take over the street, and the very children who hammered and painted on their new home might be drawn into a deadly enterprise. A Habitat house can, unfortunately, turn into a crack house. In other words, the activity that seemed so right, so charitable, may yield outcomes no one ever intended, no one even *imagined*. Measuring outcomes assumes a long view and a long accountability.

Measuring outcomes also grounds a plan in reality. Inspiring visions tend to take the form of sweeping and grandiose claims—like eliminating poverty or ridding our streets of crime. Inspiration is important, to be sure. It's one of my favorite tools for motivating people to action. But in order for a vision to gain traction, rhetoric has to yield to reality. Poverty or crime must be quantified: How poor is poor? How many break-ins do we have now, and how many would we see as a substantial improvement? How many families at what income level would the proposed program elevate, and to what level, and for how long? No investor in his or her right mind, no reasonable taxpayer for that matter, believes that a program—

any program—could eliminate poverty from our land. Or crime. We must be satisfied with incremental change. In more tightly focused efforts with a narrowly defined population or boundary, we might expect dramatic results. Like the 54 percent drop in crime that took place within two years of tearing down and redesigning the housing project in East Lake, one of the Atlanta neighborhoods FCS partnered with. (More on that project in chapter 7.) But eliminate crime or poverty? No, outcome goals must have the ring of reason if they are to attract funding and support.

Another by-product of measuring outcomes is the intelligence gained about what works, and why. In South Atlanta, for instance, we expected to see a significant drop in crime as we implemented our community transformation strategy. We closed down a liquor store that had blighted the community. We recruited dozens of "strategic neighbors" to move into the neighborhood. We organized crime watches and strengthened alliances with local police. We eliminated several crack houses. The neighborhood appeared to be on the upswing. And yet reported crime continued to escalate. We were baffled. A closer investigation by our independent researchers brought several contributing factors to the surface. For one thing, there were now more valuables to steal. New neighbors brought in new cars, expensive sound systems, computers. But the main reason for the increase was that there were more people *reporting* criminal activity. For years, low-income renters had simply resigned themselves to the illegal activity on their streets.

They tolerated the drugs, the petty theft, the muggings. Only the most severe offences—violent rape, murder, vicious attacks on seniors—were reported. Now arriving on the scene were active, vested young homeowners committed to turning the community into a healthy environment to raise their kids in. They would not tolerate blatant lawlessness. And so the reporting of every sort of illegal activity increased dramatically. Thus crime statistics skyrocketed in the community, especially during the first two years, while the newly energized leadership struggled to get the upper hand on street crime.

Some might surmise from the tone of the preceding paragraphs that I am a results-oriented person. They would be correct. I must admit that I have a diminishing appreciation for those who gauge their effectiveness by the number of food boxes they hand out or the number of recipients who visit their clothes closets. This kind of charity values *output* over *outcome*. It responds to an immediate need (often unverified) with little concern about the longer-term dependent and deceitful relationships it might foster.

Authentic relationships are fundamental to effective ministry—relationships built upon trust and reciprocity rather than hand-down giving. I will be the first to admit, however, that such service can be difficult to measure. In my early days of youth work, the youth ministry that hired me was quite concerned with numbers—number of schools, number of kids at events, number of decisions for Christ. My numbers always looked bad. I was working with a particular subgroup: kids from the juvenile court, kids with behavior problems, kids who required megadoses of personal attention. Unlike the school-oriented students who flocked to our organization's social events (good numbers), my kids needed individualized treatment. A group of a dozen was as much as I could handle. The cost per kid was high, and the decisions for Christ low. It took much longer to establish trust with untrusting delinquents, and even then the behavior changes were sporadic at best. The stories of street kids rescued from a life of crime were few and far between, and usually disappointingly short-lived. It took years, many years, of consistent caring to see the fruit of the investments made in the lives of these troubled young people. A precious few could be legitimately claimed as successes.

How, then, do you measure outcomes in high-touch ministries like mentoring, tutoring, coaching? The short-term results are pretty obvious: goal setting, improved grades, teamwork. The longer-term outcomes, however, are far less predictable. The kids you had highest hopes for are often the ones who disappoint you the most, and the ones who gave you the most trouble may be the very ones who turn out the best. Perhaps this is the ultimate test of the "unconditionality" of our love. We remain a consistent friend over time, regardless of the decisions recipients have made. Unconditional *love* does not mean, however, that there are no conditions on our *relationship*. Tough love, in the form of if-then contingencies, is essential to a respectful, responsible relationship. Though we may not be able to control direct outcomes, we can certainly control the boundaries and consistency of a relationship—essentials to fostering health.

While we're on the subject of relationships, I should say a word about a "ministry of presence." Just being a good neighbor, being available to lend a tool or watch a neighbor's kids, being active in a neighborhood watch—this presence is a vitally important ministry that doesn't lend itself to specific measured outcomes. Simply being with someone at, say, a time of tragedy or grief can be very healing. As a matter of fact, in my own times of deep personal loss I did not want others to try to *do* anything for me or even *say* comforting words. Just being there was enough. Disciplined silence and intentional inactivity, gifts given from a sensitive heart, can be extremely meaningful.

A "ministry of presence," however, is quite different from programs and services intended to assist those in need. Helping strategies, if indeed they are to be ultimately helpful, demand careful examination of long-term implications. There is no guarantee that unexamined charity will have a redemptive outcome simply because it "seems right" or feels good to the giver. As we have seen, caring people can become unintentional obstacles to the growth of the very ones they desire to help—even if their care is offered in the name of Christ. Scattering ten thousand well-intentioned volunteers across a city may not be the most redemptive or responsible strategy, as it turns out.

CHAPTER FIVE

Meeting Market Demands

NICARAGUA IS A LUSH TROPICAL land with awe-inspiring volcanoes, abundant lakes, fertile soil, stunning coastline views—and grinding poverty. Centuries of conflict and ravages of nature have reduced its capital, Managua, to a sprawling barrio. No manicured town square framed with historic buildings, no modern skyscrapers, no tree-lined boulevards— just miles of drab, squat buildings and tin-roofed shacks laced together with a confusing network of potholed streets and dirt alleys. From a ten-thousand-foot approach, the smog from cooking fires, belching diesel engines, and tens of thousands of smoke-spewing motorcycles obscures the view of the city. At three thousand feet you can make out the fenced boundaries of La Chureca, the smoldering city dump with its convoys of garbage trucks and swarms of human scavengers.

At ground level, the fourteen hundred dwellers of La Chureca (literally, "the dump") ignore the pollution. These "dump people," as they are known, survive by foraging glass, plastic, aluminum, and other discarded junk. They live in hovels constructed from materials gleaned from the castoffs of the city. From all appearances they are the most wretched of the poor in a poverty-stricken country.

A Texas church group on a mission trip to Nicaragua recently wanted to see for themselves the on-ground conditions at La Chureca. What they saw touched them deeply: ill-clad urchins combing through mountains of garbage, hoping to find enough saleable rubbish to trade for a morsel of food; women dragging heavy bags of trash to makeshift sorting areas; men scooping up armfuls of heaping refuse. How could they survive the filth, the stench, the disease? These images were burned indelibly into the conscience of the compassionate visitors.

Something simply *had* to be done, the Texans concluded. Something significant, something more than typical service project activities or suitcases full of clothes—something that would permanently change the lives, the future, of these desperately poor people. Clearly, it would require drastic intervention to release them from this enslavement.

The Texans returned home, but they didn't forget. Over the following months, they organized a task force, assembled a plan, raised money, bought rural land, and designed a new, wholesome community for the people of La Chureca, far from the stench of the refuse pit. Each little home would have enough land to grow food to feed a family. Surrounding acreage of rich volcanic soil would yield agricultural produce sufficient, when sold, to enable the entire village to thrive. In this healthy rural environment parents could pursue time-honored farming traditions while their children breathed clean air, bathed in and drank ample pure water, and developed their minds at a nearby school. The vision of dramatic transformation was absolutely intoxicating!

Hundreds of volunteers mobilized around the project, both back home and in Nicaragua. Architects designed, engineers researched, marketers promoted, planners organized. Energy was high and money flowed. Soon dozens of houses were springing out of the ground, sturdy little homes that would protect against the monsoon winds and rains. The modest construction cost was held even lower by all the volunteer hands—less than $12,000 per house!

The mood at the dedication ceremony was euphoric. Scores of volunteers flew in for the event. Emotional prayers of thanksgiving were lifted heavenward. Praise music reverberated from loudspeakers. Smiling "New La Chureca" families in their freshly donated clothes posed proudly in front of their homes. It seemed that a new era had begun for them.

Two years later all the families were living back at the dump!

Why would families that had finally gained access to shelter and clean water give up those essentials to return to their previous, squalid lives? Part of the reason was financial. They were able to sell their rural homes, albeit for a fraction of their worth. Another part was psychological: people are comfortable with what they're familiar with. Homeless folks who are finally given a bed at a shelter often still sleep on the floor, since sleeping on the ground is what they're used to.

La Chureca isn't an anomaly, either. A mission group recently returning from Haiti recounted a similar experience. Moved by compassion on seeing mothers carrying infants wrapped in dirty rags and newspapers, they purchased blankets and distributed them to the mothers. The following day, the blankets appeared in the shops along the street, having been sold by the mothers to local merchants. Discovering the babies again swaddled in filth, the missionaries were highly incensed.

What's wrong with these people!?

Perhaps there is something in a culture of poverty, something inherently defective, that restrains progress—something that we as achievers do not fully grasp. Or perhaps it is simply a resignation to the inevitable, a conditioning that enables people to endure unending oppression or the realities of a barren environment. For some reason (or multiple reasons), these poverty cultures seem incapable of leveraging the opportunities and resources provided to them to raise their standard of living. Even the billions in microloans that are now accessible in almost every depressed region of the world seem to do little to move the poverty needle.

Asking what's wrong with these people is certainly one line of inquiry. Another tack would be to examine our methods of service, as well as the assumptions that guide this service. Turns out the people of La Chureca had no use for farms or donated homes, because urban recycling had supported their community for generations. They were recyclers, not farmers; the village many outsiders disdainfully called La Chureca, *they* proudly called Los Martinez. As for the Haitian mothers, the missionaries there later learned that the women had sold the donated blankets to purchase food. The mothers needed to feed their children; they weren't concerned with blankets.

Instead of trying to figure out the method to poverty's madness, maybe we should start taking stock of our own maddening methods. An honest "What's wrong with *us*?" might shed some light on the reasons why poverty so stubbornly persists. If we probe a bit deeper, we are likely to discover that *we're* the ones to blame, like the shopkeeper who goes out of business because he's selling the wrong merchandise to the wrong clientele. Here it's useful to start with an age-old business adage: "Give the people what they want, where they want it."

Adapting one's mission to the priorities of the poor is key to redemptive service. Repairing a widow's rotting porch may not be as important as getting her water turned back on. To determine the true hierarchy of need, enough time must be spent among the needy to understand the daily survival pressures they face. A successful business understands the importance of listening to the consumer. And it's high time nonprofits started listening to the people they're trying to serve.

When I was six, I heard an advertisement on the radio about how easily and quickly one could learn to play a harmonica. I was captivated. I begged my mother to help me order one. I would pay for it, I assured her, from my allowance savings. After weeks of checking the mailbox, I finally pulled out my harmonica. It was a colossal disappointment. The instrument was made of cheap plastic and the instructions were difficult to read. It was immediately obvious to my six-year-old mind that all my blowing was never going to produce melodious tunes like those I had heard on the radio advertisement.

To ease my wounded spirit (and perhaps to encourage my musical interest), my parents gave me a really nice harmonica for my next birthday. A metal one that sounded harmonious no matter where a person blew on its keyboard. And blow I did. I practiced and practiced, mostly on simple church tunes, but also a few faster-moving ones like "Turkey in the Straw."

Back then, my church was big on revival. We prayed fervently every Sunday for another "great awakening." That's what the country really needed, we were told—a spiritual outpouring that would save us from all the evil and immorality that were rampant in our society. I once asked my mother how to start a revival. Prayer, she counseled me—lots of prayer. Prayer and obedience. Do whatever God asks of us, she said.

Six-year-old minds are very active, and mine was no different. I pondered what *I* could do to help start a revival and save our land, since congregational prayers seemed to be needing some reinforcement. What if I offered God my harmonica-playing ability? "Could God use *that* to start a revival?" I asked my mother. She said that it was a wonderful idea, that God can use any gift offered to accomplish his purposes.

Sixty-six years later the lessons I gleaned from my harmonica days are still with me. I remain highly suspicious of anyone selling anything that seems too good to be true. But I do believe what my mother told me—at least the part about God's being able to use any gift offered to accomplish his purposes. And another conviction remains—the belief that everyone, including six-year-olds, has an innate desire to make a difference in the world.

This is why young people sign up for mission trips. And because we know this, we play to this desire in our recruitment appeals. The alluring message remains "*You* can save the world." It has enormous heart-appeal. And what parents can resist the impulses of their child's heart to make a difference in the world? But do mission trips overpromise the actual results? Will this quick and easy method of ministry lead to the same kind of colossal disappointment as the deceptive harmonica hype I fell for?

Recently I received an e-mail from a young woman who asked for my counsel on conducting responsible volunteer mission work, especially for youth. She regularly coordinated mission trips to Haiti. She was painfully aware that the service her volunteers performed was largely make-work, and that their suitcases stuffed with free gifts only perpetuated a hands-out mentality among Haitians.

Her concern was a legitimate one—one that troubles many of us involved in mission work. And although I share her concerns, I also understand the demand for youth-focused mission trips and the pressure to continue planning them. We all do. Exposing young adults to the needs of the world and the amazing work of God in harsh environments is important ministry. It opens their eyes, stirs their hearts, and draws them into compassionate action. That's why mission trips can be significant in the spiritual development of our youth. And that's what mission trips should be about—spiritual development, not saving the world. Not immediately, anyway. They're about saving *us*. Preparing *us*. Once that is clear, we can venture into Haiti and other places of need with integrity.

We all desire to develop inspired and inspiring young leaders, not disillusioned ones. It is certainly important for young people (of all ages) to believe deeply that they can make a difference in their world. It is important for them to know that in God's economy *every* act of love counts—every smile, every kind word, every thoughtful deed. In my mom's words: "God can use any gift offered to accomplish his purposes." But it is also important for young people to understand how helping can sometimes hurt. Passing out T-shirts and candy to excited village children may seem like pure kindness until volunteers learn that this only encourages a culture of beggary. Eager to serve, missionaries innocently offer to do things for others, not realizing that they have wounded the pride and dignity of people who have more than adequate capability to do those things for themselves.

Every mission-tripper must understand, then, that we go to learn, not to save. The mindset of learners is very different from that of servers. Learners listen to others; servers do for others. Learners ask questions; servers offer answers. Learners marvel at the faith of the poor; servers pity the poor. Learners see ingenuity; servers see poverty. Learners affirm the worth of people; servers diminish their dignity. You see where I am going with this?

We cannot serve people out of poverty *at all*! If we expect the poor to become self-sufficient—to develop their own support systems, here and abroad—we must partner with them to create wealth based on *their* expectations and *their* way of life, not ours. This brings me finally to my response to the young woman's e-mail: How do these realities affect how we do mission—especially mission trips for youth?

First of all, our marketing to potential mission recruits has to have integrity. The proposed trip is primarily about *us*, not *them*. And that's okay. This is an insight trip to expand our spiritual horizons, see how faith works when resources are severely limited, discover how God is at work among culturally and theologically diverse people. Such insights can be transformative. They can, in fact, become the very catalysts that ignite a ministry calling.

Second, we are not on a mission to help the poor by distributing suitcases full of giveaways or performing meaningless make-work or assuming roles that can better be handled by locals. We do not promote beggary. We engage in exchange, economic as well as interpersonal. We enjoy the hospitality extended by our hosts, and we contribute to their economy by participating in the legitimate enterprise of tourism through fair payment for food, lodging, local transportation, and preparation time. And we buy their products.

Third, we prepare our youth for the learning experience. We have them read books on effective service and articles on the host country, its history and contemporary issues. Because learning another's language honors that other, we encourage participants to master at least some key phrases in the host language. We talk about "appreciative inquiry" techniques, note-taking, and journaling. We offer regular group reflection times during and following the trip, to help youth assimilate and internalize what they are experiencing.

Fourth, we make on-the-ground connections with seasoned, in-country practitioners. This is essential if our young people are to understand the context, scope, and impact of the work. Having young mission-trippers visit with several different ministries will broaden their perspective. After all, those in-country folks are the ones who can arrange discussions with residents as well as fun activities like a soccer game with local teens. Local leaders will be relieved that they don't have to set up work projects for your group. Remember, their mission is not to be tour guides. Generous compensation for their invaluable time hosting and coordinating schedules would be most appropriate.

The God-given desire to relieve suffering and come to the aid of victims of hardship should certainly be affirmed and encouraged. But to care well requires preparation. Learning precedes effective helping. And integrity simply *must* direct our marketing.

Just like unscrupulous harmonica hype can make an innocent boy feel ripped off, so can the overpromised impact of service projects disillusion enthusiastic young hearts. Rightly promoted and structured, however, mission trips can be some of our best training ground for a lifetime of effective service.

Misallocation of Funds

OUR MISSION BUDGETS ARE at an all-time high, and yet our full-time missionaries are at a hundred-year low. It's worth asking, then: How is this new arrangement working?

In terms of cost-effectiveness, the present system is abysmal. The two million short-term missionaries the Western church deploys annually consume somewhere between $3.5 and $5 billion of our overall mission expenditure. A Delta Air Lines official recently told me that a full half of their Central and South American flights would have to be terminated if not for the traffic coming and going on mission trips. Our mission budgets may well be at an all-time high, but Delta is getting a sizable chunk of that money.

And how are the partnerships working on the ground? Juan Iello, president of one of Nicaragua's most successful microlending ministries, told me that there are entire sections of his country where he is unable to provide any microloans. It's not an accident that these areas are the same ones with a high concentration of U.S. church partnerships. "They are turning my people into beggars!" Juan declared with great emotion. "My people say, 'Why do we want to borrow money? The churches give it to us. Why do we want to borrow money to build a church? They build it for us.'"

The more mature U.S. mission partners understand the danger of dependency. They emphasize the importance of mutual relationships. Though they are still willing to spend the majority of their mission dollars on airfare, they refrain from giving money directly to their indigenous partners. They feel good about training and volunteering but prefer relationship-building activities over financial support. After mutual relationships have been built, loans or matching gifts may be acceptable as start-up investments for orphanages or health clinics or schools. Such grants may be on a multiyear basis but on a declining scale, to ensure local self-sufficiency. And sometimes such grants work. But often, when the missionaries have gone home, there develop misunderstandings over how the money is being spent, concerns over inadequate financial management, disagreements about mission priorities, dissatisfaction over leadership capabilities and communication. There is a fine line between accountability and control. It is hard to maintain a good partnership when you are half a world away.

Value differences may be the most difficult challenge to forming lasting partnerships. In this country, when a manager or trusted employee uses the resources of an organization for his or her own personal gain, an ethical red flag immediately begins to wave. Approved perks, such as a company car, may be perfectly acceptable. But unauthorized misallocation of funds is seen as crossing the line. Embezzling or outright theft is cause for immediate firing. That reflects American business ethics. But, in other lands, ethics are often different. In some cultures, for instance, skimming some of the unguarded assets of a wealthy company from the top is expected, because every Western-funded organization is considered wealthy.

The Opportunity Nicaragua board discovered this when we told employees at our Nicaragua food-processing operation that they could be fired for embezzling funds. They were incredulous. There seemed to be no ethical issue in *their* minds with an employee taking money from the company. A rich company can always get more money—what's the big deal? they figured. These sorts of value differences can make cross-cultural partnerships a real challenge. They are difficult enough to negotiate when cross-cultural partners are working *together* every day. But successful long-distance cross-cultural partnerships, at least in the absence of highly accountable systems, are really quite rare.

Could it be time to reconsider our romantic notions of partnership? International business practices have taught us that careful oversight (call it control) is essential. France' and Michael Allen spent two years living on-site in Mexico while launching the first international branch of their U.S.-based Ventura manufacturing company. Even now, three years later, every morning at 9:07 they have live Skype reporting from each of their local and international managers. They learned through experience that detailed reporting, daily communication, tight controls, and frequent visits are essential for good business—especially when that business crosses over cultural lines. Would we call this economic colonialism? I don't think so. I think we would call it sound business practice.

Should healthy co-venturing with ministry partners be any less rigorous? Is it not healthy ministry practice to have trusted, capable managers on the ground to ensure that the ventures we fund will be well conceived, well planned, well structured, and well led? Careful management does not imply, "We know what's best for these people" or "We can do it better than they can" or "We don't trust them." Rather, it communicates that we are serious enough about the work to invest not only our dollars, but our best talent and expertise as well. This is called responsible investment. It's time to replace the short-term mission-trip fad with a longer-term missionary strategy and convert our so-called partnerships into true *teamwork* rather than minimally accountable one-way giving.

How to Meet Market Demands

LET ME ILLUSTRATE THE lesson of how to meet market demands through a familiar picture.

Visualize a young woman recently out of seminary, working in a large church that has an ample budget. Her title is missions pastor. Spiritual nurture is her assignment. Her specific job is to educate, motivate, and mobilize church members to engage personally in mission of various sorts. She weaves mission content into the Christian education curriculum and preaches it from the pulpit from time to time. She orchestrates the church's mission conference, forms small-group discussion sessions, leads mission trips, and coordinates service projects. She develops relationships with missionaries and pastors in remote mission fields, screens local nonprofit ministries as suitable sources for volunteer involvement, and coordinates outreach and service programs. Her success is measured by the number of church members that become personally engaged in mission, and by the fulfillment that they experience participating in mission efforts. She fills an essential role in any growing, dynamic Western church.

She knows better than most what it takes to create meaningful service projects and mission trips for her members. First and foremost, she knows, the experience must address a pressing need. It is not enough to simply do make-work; a worthwhile experience must accomplish real and lasting good. Cleaning up a vacant city lot or painting a Honduran church might work for youth, but adults with a life's worth of wisdom under their belt need something of much greater significance. Like establishing a medical clinic for a disease-plagued village, or something else that would really make a difference.

Thus the activities the missions pastor promotes must be life-changing, either for the people being served or for the ones doing the serving, but hopefully for both. While it is exceedingly rare for a one-day service project or a one-week mission trip to deliver life-changing results, volunteers must be made to understand that even their small investments will produce significant results. Painting a picture of the importance of service is an important part of the missions pastor's duty.

This is not spin, however. This is conviction. The missions pastor believes in her heart that one-day service projects and one-week mission trips really do make a difference. She believes that in the economy of God every act of kindness, no matter how small, has redemptive impact. Even when you cannot see the results. She teaches her parishioners this. And she is right, of course. God's economy is different from the human economy. The widow's mite is more valuable than the queen's gold. In the kingdom of God, the sacrifice of a Saturday or a week of selfless service has untold value. It is the missions pastor's job—her calling—to affirm the compassionate motivation and genuine goodness of her people.

But she is caught in a tension. A number of tensions, really. One has to do with numbers. Numbers are important—number of volunteers, number of projects, number of mission trips, number of food boxes distributed, number of ministries supported. Numbers are one of the criteria upon which her performance is evaluated. But quantity does not necessarily equal quality. A horde of youth descending on an inner-city neighborhood for a clean-up day may not be as effective as a select group of high school students who tutor grade-schoolers for a semester. Both activities may be good, but their impact is significantly different. Activities are not the same as outcomes, as we have seen. And, in many instances, smaller is better.

Another tension she lives in involves competing agendas. Her charge is to "educate, motivate, and mobilize church members to engage personally in mission." This is not the same as elevating the poor out of poverty (which is what much service claims to be about). These two agendas—mobilizing members and elevating the poor—may converge in a well-conceived service project or mission trip. But the missions pastor's first and foremost responsibility is the spiritual nurture of her people. Service is a means to an end. The temptation, the tendency—indeed the mandate of her employment—is to plan activities that suit the needs of the servers rather than address the deeper (and often more complex) needs of those being served. Viewed in that light, leading a week of summer vacation Bible school in Guatemala is preferable to starting a business enterprise that enables Guatemalan youth to emerge from poverty. Sometimes good becomes the enemy of best. The missions pastor must live in this tension.

Yet another tension grows out of finances. Service is expensive—especially mission trips. Because parents and friends are usually supportive when teenagers express compassionate interest in others, money for mission adventures is relatively easy to raise. But raising money is not the problem. Return on investment is. The missions pastor knows that the costs are high compared to the actual work being done— typically, very high. She knows that there is no way to justify that kind of expenditure except as the cost of spiritual development for her own people. But that is not how the trip is being sold to mission-trippers and their generous supporters. It is billed as "spreading the gospel" or "loving the unloved" or "rescuing the perishing"—none of which is really truthful.

Perhaps the most troubling tension, however, lies in perpetuating a dishonesty for the sake of protecting the feelings of some of her most loyal members. She knows that her integrity is compromised when she affirms the service of volunteers, knowing all the while that their work is actually doing as much harm as (or more harm than) good. She sees quite clearly that the poor who get clothes from the church's clothes closet and food from the food pantry are "repeat customers."

She knows in her heart that unhealthy dependencies have

developed, that some recipients are using these benevolences to support a destructive lifestyle. And she has witnessed first-hand similar outcomes among the poor of remote villages that her mission-trip recruits have visited: she has seen well-intended benevolence foster a culture of beggary and weaken the capacity for self-sufficiency. But how is she to convey this concern to the dedicated servants who give selflessly of their time collecting and sorting clothes, boxing donated food, and distributing "necessities of life" to "the least of these" as acts of compassion and obedience to their Lord? Or to those who have given up weeks of their time and raised thousands of dollars to serve the poor in foreign lands? How can she tell them that their good and righteous efforts are doing harm? Does she continue to protect their feelings with half-truths, or does she risk telling them the whole story?

A sensitive (and smart) missions pastor knows better than to launch a frontal assault. The damage could be far-reaching, extending well beyond the wounded spirits of a few dedicated saints. She finds a more politically savvy means to enlighten her people. She discusses the matter with her senior pastor, perhaps, and secures his support to initiate a discussion with her missions committee. She introduces that committee to a book that has recently been recommended to her—one that has been stirring up a lot of discussion in churches of their denomination. (*When Helping Hurts* or *Toxic Charity* will do just fine.) She wants her leaders to be on the cutting edge of missions, to adopt an affirming approach to change. She leads them through a book study that surfaces all the issues she has been quietly struggling with.

As her missions committee begins to grapple with these realities, she suggests to the chairman that it might be instructive to conduct an evaluation of current practices to determine the effectiveness of their outreach. Meanwhile, she explores best practices of other churches that offer creative alternatives to hurtful outcomes of traditional charity. As candid discussions lead to questions about change, she has models to introduce and site visits to suggest. She knows that the process will take time. She does not try to rush it. But it will be her gentle, persistent nudges (and those of her more progressive leaders) that will ultimately convert their missions program from toxic to transformative.

CHAPTER SIX

Reciprocal Exchange

FOOD

We understand the importance of successful business practices. How then do we employ them in the battle against poverty and its attendant problems? Why not start with the universal need for food, an enduring problem most every church and charitable organization is quite familiar with.

As I described in chapter 1, starvation is a crisis; hunger is chronic. When famine sweeps a land, starvation becomes an urgent, life-or-death situation for huge numbers of people. Emergency food supplies must be rushed in without delay to save lives. That influx of food is an emergency response to a crisis situation. It is, for starvation, the appropriate intervention.

Hunger, though, is a different matter. In a stable nation such as the United States, which enjoys abundant supplies of food and adequate government subsidies, food insecurity is the reality of the less advantaged. Occasional hunger; not starvation. Starvation is an emergency or crisis issue. And hunger, a chronic issue of poverty, requires different strategies—different from those appropriate to starvation, and different from the ones currently in play in the United States. While distributing free food is an appropriate *emergency* response, it is seldom an appropriate response to chronic food insecurity. It may seem compassionate at the moment to give out food boxes, but in all likelihood this type of emergency response will ultimately prove more hurtful than helpful. So why do we persist in doing it?

For one thing, it feels like the right thing to do. When someone says he or she is hungry, our hearts tell us to give food, as does the Bible. Another reason is that it is much easier to take a few cans of food to church for the monthly food drive than to get personally involved with a needy family. And besides, food pantries lend themselves to volunteer participation, which is good for the church. The list could go on. But the *primary* reason we persist in giving free food to the poor is that we have wrongly assessed their need. We have assumed that their food shortage is a crisis. It is not.

What free-food advocates such as Feed America promote these days is food security—that is, all people at all times having access to enough food to sustain an active, healthy life. Roughly

15 percent of our country's population is food-insecure at least sometime during the year. Even though four out of five of these households receive food support from the government, there are still times when their cupboards are bare.

Heart-touching commercials by Feed America would have us believe that food insecurity is a crisis issue. It is not—at least not in this country. It is a chronic problem, a function of chronic poverty. Unlike the Great Depression of the 1930s, when one in four of our workers stood in bread lines with no government safety net to rescue them, today well over 90 percent of our workforce is employed, and our public subsidies are adequate.

Obviously, the need for food is forever with us. And it's persistent: every couple of hours, our bodies remind us to fuel up. Ignore the need and our stomachs begin to growl in dissatisfaction. From the time we enter the world, this need dominates our lives—and, during those early years, the lives of our parents, who must schedule their sleep around it. Mothers all over the world spend generous portions of their days preparing food for their families. Indeed, eating is fundamental to life.

Given that food is a critical priority, why in the biblical account did such a huge number of curiosity-seekers stream out into the remote countryside—without packing lunches—to see a Galilean rabbi rumored to be a miracle-worker, as the Bible describes in John 6? Some said the rabbi was the long-awaited messiah. And if that proved to be true, he would be even greater than Moses, who had provided free food (in the form of manna) for the entire Jewish nation for forty years. And, sure enough, to everyone's delight, the miracle-working rabbi came through. He took the sack lunch of a little boy (whose practical mother had planned ahead) and multiplied it before the onlooking crowd. It was a picnic the likes of which no one had ever witnessed before. All the people ate until they were stuffed, and still there were mounds of leftovers.

The following day the crowds showed up again—city people from Capernaum, village people from the region, and boatloads of folks who had ferried in from across the lake. The word was out. This could be it—the leader they had long awaited! The constant stress of securing daily bread might be alleviated at last. They pressed in around him, listening patiently to his message, watching as he laid hands on the sick, waiting with intensity for him to produce the day's supply of food. But when food was not forthcoming, the people started to become impatient.

Jesus was a little short of patience himself. "You're not following me because you believe my message or even because of the miracles I do," he said, in effect. "You're just wanting another free lunch."

"Do a miracle like Moses did—free food for everyone," the crowd demanded. "That's how you can prove you're the one sent from God."

But when it finally became apparent that the miracle-worker was not going to supply any more food, the people grew indifferent to his message. He could give them true bread from heaven that would satisfy their hunger permanently, he told them. A few were curious enough to inquire how to obtain that bread, but when he tried to explain that *he was* that bread, even they turned and walked away.

Sound familiar? A similar scenario plays out on downtown street corners every day, when a van full of volunteers pulls up with free sandwiches. Hordes of homeless suddenly emerge from alleyways and bridges, hands outstretched for whatever their benefactors are currently passing out. Are they interested in the bread of life? Try gathering them with a gospel message from a bullhorn instead of with a sandwich, and watch your numbers go down. Who wouldn't choose dependency on a predictable, visible source of food over an elusive faith-walk that offers no immediate, tangible guarantees? A sandwich in hand will win out every time over a give-us-this-day-our-daily-bread faith-prayer.

So why did the miracle-working rabbi feed the crowd in the first place? Compassion, perhaps? A *heart-response* to hungry people is certainly a divine impulse. Heart-responses don't examine recipients' motivations or project future outcomes. They see a need and take immediate action, no questions asked. But the kingdom that this radical young rabbi was introducing was about far more than heart-responses. It was about *heart-changes*. And feeding the multitudes was clearly *not* the most effective method to achieve heart-changes.

Heart-responses produce distinctly different behavior patterns than heart-changes. Continued heart-responses yield diminishing returns:

Feed a person once, it elicits appreciation.

Feed him twice, it creates anticipation.

Feed him three times, it creates expectation.

Feed him four times, it becomes an entitlement.

Feed him five times, it produces dependency.

Heart-changes, on the other hand, move a person who is currently down on his or her luck in a radically different direction. Reliance upon God increases. Dependence on God for daily bread—for body as well as soul—becomes integral to one's faith journey. Giving to others takes precedence over getting for oneself. Sharing replaces hoarding. Isolation diminishes. Community increases.

These were the values that the young rabbi wanted the people to understand and embrace. It became clear to Jesus's disciples that a free-food distribution program was not the preferred method for ushering in this new kingdom. Should it not be as obvious to us?

Innovative Models of Exchange

WANT TO CREATE A stampede? Just announce that free food is being passed out. One megachurch on Atlanta's north side found that out one recent Christmas. They collected tons of food and broadcast a public announcement of the time and place that it would be given out, first-come first-served. The city is *still* talking about the horrific traffic jams, with cars from as far away as Alabama clogging major arteries, even the interstate. Police were overwhelmed, firefighters and emergency response teams were paralyzed, and business along downtown streets ground to a halt. This wonderful, but as it turned out, naive, idea of "feeding the five thousand" at Christmastime failed to take into account the nearly irresistible power of "I've got to get mine" greed that is triggered by the lure of getting something free.

I found this out when the urban church I was a member of first opened a clothes closet. Partnering churches had donated a generous collection of gently used clothes. With loving hands and compassionate hearts, volunteers sized and arranged a spacious room full of clothes, readying it for our neighbors, who would at the appointed time be invited to partake of this generosity. Our first clue that the gracious spirit of the givers might not be shared by the recipients was the impatient elbowing and jostling for position in the line that formed outside the clothes closet on opening day. Our fears were confirmed when we opened the doors.

Our "freely given, freely received" approach collapsed as recipients rushed in, snatching and grabbing as many stacks of garments as they could wrap their arms around. With no limits, the giveaway became a chaotic free-for-all. Order was restored by the next time we opened, owing to hastily drafted rules which we posted, but the atmosphere was anything but amiable. For one thing, our one-visit-per-month, three-garments-per-visit restrictions quickly became obstacles recipients tried to circumvent. Instead of being hospitable friends to neighbors whom we came to serve, we turned into enforcers of greed-curbing regulations—not at all the relationship-building ministry we had intended!

What is it in the human psyche that innately leaps at the opportunity to get something for nothing? Videotapes of urban riots catch average citizens looting storefronts when they see others snatching and running—not criminals or thieves, just ordinary people seized by the impulse to get their share. Similarly, conservative, pinstripe-suited bankers can get caught up in the feeding frenzy of a real estate boom they know to be highly unethical if not downright illegal. There is something about the lure of free or easily gotten treasure that appeals to the baser nature of humankind.

Legitimate *exchange*, however, is different. Bargaining may stir up emotions, to be sure—though of an entirely different sort. The basis for honest trading assumes parity. One person has something of value that is desired by another. Each hopes to gain from the deal. Either can walk away if a satisfactory agreement cannot be reached. When a fair exchange is negotiated, both leave with a feeling of satisfaction. That's how the market works.

Clipping coupons, watching ads, searching the web—it's the way Americans find their bargains. Recently my wife, Peggy, came home all excited after a day of shopping. Displaying her treasures for me to admire, she proudly announced, "I saved more than I spent!" What's not to love about a bargain? It benefits both the customer who buys something and the merchant who sells it. Legitimate exchange is good for everyone.

There's a world of difference between bargains and handouts. Bargains create satisfied customers; handouts create adversarial relationships. Bargains appeal to frugality; handouts encourage hoarding. Bargains generate healthy economic exchange; handouts produce unhealthy dependency. Bargains engender pride; handouts deplete dignity.

Lest we become hardhearted, however, let's consider some responses to chronic hunger that are both helpful and equitable.

Austin and Ginny Hunt know from personal childhood experience the indignity of being in need. They understand the trap of dependency that can rob one's dignity and deepen one's despair. But they also know the importance of emergency help in times of crisis. So they set about developing an innovative system that addresses both short-term assistance and longer-term development. In 2003, they launched Harvest Food and Outreach Center to serve struggling families in their community. The program solicits donations of food and other goods from manufacturers and wholesalers and the occasional retailer. Harvest Food and Outreach Center then sells these goods to qualified store members at a deeply discounted price, approximately 30 percent of retail. While most food banks require that surplus food be *given* to needy recipients and forbid any form of exchange, Harvest believes that exchange is good for everyone. Proceeds from sales not only pay for the program's operational costs but also provide support services for qualified members, who enjoy huge savings while at the same time contributing financially to the very services that provide them a path out of poverty.

One obstacle that the Hunts had to overcome was the concern of corporate donors that selling goods at such a deeply discounted rate might pose unfair competition to their own supermarkets. But when the Hunts explained that their center was located in a low-income community not served by any supermarkets, the concern about undercutting the business of major chain stores largely disappeared. If there's anything that corporate decision-makers understand it is the value of exchange; it resonates with the idea of everyone pulling their own weight.

The community food bank, however—an organization serving the same clientele as Harvest—had concerns about competition. When name-brand food producers began to redirect their surplus merchandise to Harvest, the food bank objected. While food banks have a corner on the distribution of not-for-sale government commodities, private-sector products are fair game, as the food bank discovered. The Harvest exchange model squarely addresses the issues of deepening dependency and loss of human dignity that American charity has long avoided. It is no wonder, then, that Harvest continues to cause a considerable stir in the food bank world.

In the meantime, the Hunts have now opened stores in three Florida cities: Vero Beach, Port Saint Lucie, and Orlando. Their eighteen-thousand-square-foot distribution center serves more than five hundred families per day. To continue enhancing supportive services, Harvest also partners with Workforce Solutions, Inc., which operates a "Passport to Prosperity" program that combines life skills education with on-the-job training for families on public assistance. And the business is all self-sustaining. By any objectively measured criteria, Harvest is moving the poverty needle.

Similarly, Birch Community Services, a creative buying club, offers its members legitimate access to surplus food. Barry and Suzanne Birch formed this nonprofit membership club for struggling families in the Portland, Oregon, area. Birch Community Services provides food, clothing, and financial training. Members pay a fifty-dollar monthly membership fee and invest volunteer hours working in the food warehouse. The program emphasizes self-reliance, and an exit strategy is planned with each member. Most graduates choose food independence over government food stamps.

Another viable exchange method is a voucher bartering

system that exchanges food (and other commodities) for work performed in the community. Community gardening is a similar strategy for sharing in the proceeds of time and labor.

Rather than fostering dependency from continued emergency responses, these and other development strategies strengthen the capacity of people in need to assume a greater measure of control and self-sufficiency over their own lives.

In our neighborhood in inner-city Atlanta, FCS has also concluded that everyone has something to contribute, that no one is so poor that they're unable to help themselves. Well, almost no one. There are seriously ill and severely traumatized people who require constant care. But everyone else has some capability to offer. Young or old, it makes no difference. Everyone has ability. For example, Moving in the Spirit, our performing arts program for urban youth, begins with preschoolers. As soon as these little ones graduate to grade school level, they're required to teach younger students the same skills they learned at that age. With each new grade, the students' responsibilities increase. By the time they are in high school, students are performing before large audiences, choreographing, designing sets and costumes, planning and raising money for their annual tour—all while continuing to mentor younger performers. They also elect one of their members each year to serve on the organization's board of directors.

Even homebound seniors in our community have something to offer. Nobody keeps a more watchful eye on the street than seniors confined to their homes. Peering out through their blinds, they observe traffic and activity on the street day and night. There are no more valuable members of a neighborhood crime-watch program than seniors. As long as they are asked. They are also very effective phone-chain participants. Checking in on each other, sounding the alert when one of them has a problem or emergency, sharing prayer requests—there are a host of important assignments that seniors with limited mobility can assume to benefit their community. But first they must be recognized as assets to the neighborhood rather than burdens or objects of pity.

So if everyone has something of worth to offer, it falls to the stewards of resources and programs to devise effective systems of reciprocal exchange. When our inner-city church made the decision to replace our free-food pantry with a food co-op, we had no idea how our former pantry recipients would respond. The co-op model we chose is a membership club in which dues-paying members receive an equal share of the biweekly food distribution. In a real sense, co-op members are owners. It is their responsibility to "shop" at the local food bank and select the appropriate quantities and varieties of food.

One of the first concerns the co-op had to deal with was the issue of credit. If a member didn't have her four-dollar dues one week, should the co-op extend her credit until she could repay her debt? Since the fellow co-op members—not the church—would assume the financial risk, a lively debate ensued. Eventually an acceptable agreement was negotiated. But in the process, members realized that they needed to codify the co-op's evolving policies, which required both a secretary to take minutes during meetings and, later, a treasurer to keep track of the co-op's ledger—those who paid, and when, and those with outstanding dues. The co-op found these talented people from the very same line that used to wrap around the church. These ample gifts had always been there, but charitable church volunteers had failed to recognize their potential for years while passing out bags of free food. Today, similarly talented and invested community residents, all of whom are former food pantry recipients, run six food co-ops with fifty households in each.

How to Change the Program

TAKE THE EXAMPLE OF one church's response to its community's food shortage. The church in question was justifiably proud of its community food pantry. Initially run out of a closet in the church basement, the pantry had turned into a spacious, well-run distribution center with its own separate building adjacent to the church. With rows of neatly stocked shelves, bins for fresh produce, and a cooler for perishables, it looked more like a small grocery store than a pantry. A state-of-the-art computer system kept track of inventory, recorded donor contributions, monitored distributions and the recipients who received them, and maintained good financial records. Local grocery stores and bakeries happily donated surplus and outdated food. Other churches contributed as well.

Though it was called "the Pantry," the full-fledged food distribution operation was run more like a business than a basement charity. It had a full-time director, a part-time bookkeeper, and several dozen regular volunteers. It was now open four days a week and served growing numbers of needy beneficiaries that streamed in from all over the county. School counselors and agency caseworkers referred clients in need of emergency assistance. Throughout the city, the Pantry had become known as an important player in its social safety net.

Then one day a church member handed the pastor a copy of *Toxic Charity*, which argued that giveaway programs such as the Pantry actually hurt the poor more than they helped. The church member called into question the validity of the centerpiece of the church's far-reaching ministry. If the book's central thesis were true, the Pantry would have to go. And not just the Pantry—the congregation's service outreach and mission trips would also have to be revamped! This is not the kind of disruption a busy pastor needs.

The pastor was faced with two options, neither of which was ideal. He could dismiss the book by building a biblical counterargument and acknowledging that, while every ministry has its flaws, that's no reason to stop serving the poor. Or he could change the entire ministry paradigm. If he chose the latter, he'd have to tell all his volunteers that their countless hours of selfless service were unhelpful, even hurtful, that all the generous donations weren't useful, but harmful. He would have to tell the families and agencies who counted on the church that they were changing the program. No, the pastor concluded: there's no way he could do *that*. The fallout would be disastrous.

But the problem wouldn't go away. It ate at the pastor's peace of mind. Isn't community service about helping the needy, he thought—not just making church members feel good? And if, as that darn book says, the way our church is doing service actually harms those we're attempting to help, then our program is clearly self-serving. And he's right. Not intentionally, of course, but in reality, this program may be more about the church's self-interest than about those being served.

If this church is going to have integrity, it cannot bury its head in the sand and assume that all is well—not after the alarm has sounded. Leaders must at least take an honest look at the outcomes of the congregation's charity. Is there really unintended harm being done? A few discreet, nondisruptive interviews with Pantry workers might give some clues. Questions like these: How often do you see the same people in the food lines? How many reports do you get back from recipients that free food has helped them over a temporary tough spot? Does the Pantry seem to encourage trusting relationships, or do we have to be on constant guard against abuse of the system? Questions like these will provide a bit of insight into whether the program is empowering recipients or simply fostering unhealthy dependency. Reassuring answers may put the issue to rest.

Or, they may raise even more questions. Questions like:

Why are there so few anecdotal success stories? Why are recipients not becoming involved in the life of the church? Why do Pantry workers seem somewhat defensive about the inquiries? Probe a little deeper and it may become apparent that, as *Toxic Charity* claims, the well-run giveaway program reeks of dependency, deception, and the depreciation of dignity. That's when the *real* problem arises—how to fix a ministry that most folks don't think is broken.

Changing an institution that is heavily vested in "the way we have always done things" is a major challenge—whether that institution is a corporation, a church, or *your* home parish. Part of a pastor's job is keeping his or her institution growing and keeping the members reasonably happy. The last thing a spiritual leader wants is to stir up divisive controversy that could alienate good and faithful members. But a spiritual leader must also have integrity. So if it becomes apparent that change is necessary to ensure responsible care for the poor, there is no alternative but to act. But how?

Certainly not a frontal assault. Too much damage could be inflicted on the "compassion corps" by declaring their good works toxic. A much subtler change strategy is needed. Distributing copies of *Toxic Charity* to key leaders (perhaps covertly) would stimulate considerable discussion. Such conversations begin working the soil.

Once the discussion is under way, arrange for key leaders to visit a few innovative models—those employing best practices—being implemented elsewhere by other ministries.

This will help move the discussion from critique to creativity. A food co-op buying club model, a bartering system, a thrift store with deeply discounted basics—such ideas that have succeeded in other places can ignite the imagination, especially of entrepreneurial types.

In addition, encourage a few key leaders to attend the Christian Community Development Association annual conference, a gathering of practitioner thought-leaders committed to assisting ministries to empower the poor. That will definitely till up some new ground. This sort of nonconfrontational exploration process is likely to plant seeds of interest in new methods of service.

Adding a new, complementary program is far less volatile than attempting to dismantle and replace an existing one. So perhaps the food pantry stays. At least for a time. But alongside it, you may choose to offer recipients the option to join a buying club co-op in which members pay four dollars biweekly (as in the example earlier in this chapter) and receive back ten to twenty times that amount in groceries. Like shareholders, members have the pride of ownership, control of food selection, and accountability to each other. Dignity replaces begging; belonging replaces impersonal food lines. One church that tried a pairing of food pantry and co-op discovered that, as co-op membership increased, food lines dwindled, until eventually almost no free food was distributed. This is just one idea. The point is, transitioning from doing *for* the poor to doing *with* them need not be disruptive or alienating. It begins with one decisive step in the right direction.

The food pantry may continue to function for years to come in that church that adopted a food co-op—just as the old and the new may coexist in any church that experiments with new ways of serving the poor—but the shift to empowerment has begun with the first step toward reciprocal exchange. A door has been opened that allows church members and recipients alike to experience firsthand the differences between the pridelessness of one-way charity and the dignity of reciprocal exchange. Outcomes will eventually become obvious. Once empowerment principles take root and spread beyond the food pantry to other areas of ministry—benevolence giving, service projects, mission trips—a paradigm of development will become the new norm.

CHAPTER SEVEN

The Three Rs of Community Development

THE VOICES ADVOCATING FOR THE poor are many and varied. Some push for increased government entitlements—more rent subsidies, food stamps, energy assistance, unemployment benefits. Some lobby for increasing the minimum wage. Others urge Congress to create more jobs. A legitimate case could be made for any of these approaches. Perhaps.

But, in my judgment, these proposed solutions are unlikely to succeed. Nudging up the minimum wage does little to move unskilled workers toward self-sufficiency. Upping entitlements *dis*empowers rather than empowers recipients. The creation of low-end jobs with no benefits and little chance for advancement offers short-term gain but does nothing to end poverty.

So if raising the minimum wage doesn't significantly move the poverty needle, and if increasing entitlements only deepens dependency, what *will* work to alleviate poverty?

What about higher education or technical training? This is certainly a step in the right direction. No argument there. But among those who beat the odds, make it into college, and succeed at a career, few ever return to their old neighborhood to share the benefit. And who could blame them? Thus, though noble, an educational approach to poverty alleviation designed to rescue one person at a time isn't good enough. It doesn't go deep enough into the underlying sources that perpetuate poverty. In order to transform the neighborhoods where the poor live, we must reweave the very fabric of the community.

John Perkins discovered this fifty years ago when he moved back to his hometown of Mendenhall, a rural community about twenty-five miles south of Jackson, Mississippi. He never expected to return to the place that had nearly claimed his life as a young civil rights activist. But a call from God changed his mind—and his direction.

To John's surprise, however, his efforts to educate and expand the horizons of young people in his hometown, while enormously beneficial to the individuals involved, proved a detriment to the community at large. Capable youth who went off to college never returned. Inadvertently, John was facilitating the outward migration of the community's best and brightest. If the town was ever going to rise from its poverty-bound past, John realized, a generation of young people would have to catch a vision for its transformation and commit themselves to a cause greater than their personal pursuit of the American dream.

So John preached that vision. His message was compelling. It captured the attention of a young generation hungry for greater meaning in their lives. This was the beginning of a powerful new movement known as the Christian Community Development Association (CCDA), which has resulted in the strategic redeployment of many thousands of visionary young adults into communities of need across the country.

Back in the 1980s, John's personal example and message influenced several of the FCS staff—my family included—to move into inner-city Atlanta and become neighbors to the kids and families in our program. The move changed the entire course of our ministry. The political suddenly became personal. Poverty and its attendants, crime and isolation, were no longer abstractions; they were an everyday struggle. We had to fight crime to keep our streets safe. We pursued adequate housing when homeless neighbors showed up on our doorstep. We quickly evolved from a youth ministry into a community development organization, expanding into family counseling and job training and education reform.

John's efforts in Mendenhall demonstrated the powerful impact that becoming neighbors can have on a community, an impact that I myself, and others across the country, later validated. From this experience emerged the three Rs of community development: *reneighboring, reconciliation,* and *redistri-*

bution. The three Rs became bedrock principles of the CCDA movement. The first of these, living among the people you serve, is essential for effective ministry.

Reneighboring

DRUG ADDICTION, MENTAL ILLNESS, a deficiency of marketable skills—they all keep the poor locked in a troubling cycle of dependency and despondency. Equally troubling, though, is isolation, which reinforces and perpetuates poverty. That isolation is revealed in terms such as "the other side of the tracks," "the ghetto," "the projects"—terms that describe those separated by railroad tracks or freeways or invisible class and racial barriers. Human services and compassionate ministries can certainly make life more tolerable for residents in these isolated communities, but real improvement takes more than service. It requires the reweaving of the social fabric of the community. The poor living in segregated neighborhoods find it difficult to get the resources they need to change their situation. Mixed-income neighbors, with their breadth of clout and ideas, are needed to improve chances for the poor. That means reneighboring.

A committed businessman turned nonprofit executive confided to me his frustration that his organization's programs weren't having much impact on the target community that he had hoped to change. "We have thirty different programs serving the needs of our community," he said, "but frankly, things aren't getting better."

It was a discouraging admission. This man, a trusted friend, had given up a successful career to minister among the poor. It was not as though he hadn't performed adequate due diligence. Like any competent business leader, he had researched the areas of need in his city, identified the target community with the most severe problems, established a list of the most pressing issues, studied best practices, visited working models, built collaborative relationships with agencies and churches serving in the area, and initiated a number of well-designed programs. He invested nearly a decade of the best years of his life attempting to improve conditions in this troubled area of town, only to come to the disheartening realization that "things aren't getting better."

Certainly he could point to some individual successes. A number of the community's youth had graduated high school and, at the time of our conversation, were enrolled in four-year colleges. A number of adults had transitioned off welfare and found gainful employment. Some families had moved out of public housing into better neighborhoods. These were all good things, the kind of stories that kept donors inspired and money flowing in.

As positive as these stories were, however, they were anecdotal—infrequent occurrences that did not reflect an overall improvement in the quality of community life. Crime still ruled the streets, unemployment was still high, teen pregnancy remained epidemic, and poverty still persisted.

"My organization has some excellent programs," he told me—and indeed they did. Their efforts were laudable; but if programs could fix communities, the community that his organization served would be showing signs of improvement. *Programs* don't fix communities; they can't. They may genuinely help some individuals (often by enabling those individuals to escape the neighborhood), but they don't bring about fundamental community change. Only *neighbors* can do that. Neighbors, after all, are the building blocks of every neighborhood. When programs empower the best and the brightest neighbors to move out, they unintentionally weaken the community.

"The only way to change a neighborhood," I told him, "is through reneighboring." It was not the answer he was expecting, but it was the only solution I knew to address the heart of the issue. Without connected, involved, resourced neighbors, no neighborhood can thrive. Without a transfusion of new blood, troubled communities will continue to deteriorate as the capable exit in pursuit of better opportunities. An infusion of new life, rich with creativity, teeming with fresh ideas and energy, abundant with capacity—this is what invigorates a community. These nonmonetary riches spawn hope among discouraged residents, giving them a reason to stay. The very presence of vested neighbors committed to ridding their streets of drugs, improving educational opportunities, and restoring homes ignites hope and kindles visions of what the community could become. Thus a vested citizenship becomes the catalyst for transformation from within.

The rub, of course, is getting middle-income residents to move into a bad neighborhood. Reneighboring obviously raises the stakes for such residents. It takes people of courage and commitment, people willing to be like those Marines who parachute in under hostile fire, secure a beachhead, then push inland and take back territory held by the enemy. Who would sign up for such hazardous duty? Many people, actually. The problem is, hardly anyone ever asks them.

"My wife would never agree to move into that neighborhood," my friend admitted. This was understandable, given the amenities she'd have to give up. But I was pretty sure *he* wouldn't be willing to make the move either. He was far too invested in his comfortable, secure lifestyle to seriously consider such a radical change. Leaving his business career to devote himself to nonprofit work was radical enough, and indeed showed great heart and determination. But because he was unable to detach from a standard of living he had worked a lifetime to provide, he felt blocked from asking others to make such a move. "Do as I say, not as I do" lacks a certain conviction, as he was well aware. And so my friend stuck with his commuter-led program model rather than daring to try an incarnational, transformation strategy.

That decision doomed his well-run programs. Why? Because for a neighborhood to flourish, it must retain indigenous leaders (*remainers*), attract fresh leaders (*relocaters*), and draw achievers (*returners*) back to the community. Good schools are essential for flourishing, but they are not sufficient, because—as John Perkins found out—people who go off to college rarely return to their under-resourced childhood communities. The same is true of other good and important programs: they are essential but not sufficient. Community transformation is about the quality of neighbors, not the quality of programs.

Diverse neighbors living together in the same community is not such a strange concept these days, certainly not as unusual as it was when I moved my family into inner-city Atlanta. As a matter of fact, mixed-income development currently has broad acceptance in the real estate development industry, as well as in municipal urban planning departments. While there is legitimate concern about the displacement of low-income residents, there is also the recognition that concentrated poverty is unhealthy for everyone. Having learned from earlier, failed attempts at what came to be derided as urban "removal"—urban renewal efforts that destroyed housing and left vacant expanses of undeveloped urban land—many local governments and the U.S. Department of Housing and Urban Development (HUD) now require one-for-one replacement housing when affordable units are torn down to build new, market-appropriate residences. When longtime residents are invited to the planning table, when they're given choices, when their needs are taken into consideration, the process of change can be just and cooperative. When intelligent minds join with sensitive hearts to devise sound strategies for economically viable community development, foundations for shalom are laid. And when new, energetic neighbors join in community life with those who have endured long years of hardship, opportunity for the dreamed-of "beloved community" is within reach.

When a mixed-income community is functioning in reasonably healthy ways, the need for externally funded programs decreases. This became quite clear the year our younger son Jonathan turned sixteen. He needed a job—or rather, we *told* him he needed a job! He decided to put in an application at Zoo Atlanta, and we approved. The zoo wasn't the highest-paying employer in the city, but it offered a wholesome working environment and supplied nice uniforms and a pith helmet. Besides, it was just a short walk from our home. Unbeknownst to Jonathan, I knew one of the senior administrators at the zoo and decided to give her a call. No special treatment, I told her; I just wanted to give her a heads-up that Jonathan was coming over. It was no great surprise that he was hired.

On his off-hours, as Jon was playing basketball with his buddies on our street, he mentioned to them that the zoo was hiring. "You ought to apply," he told them. "Put me down as a reference." Within two weeks, four of his friends also had jobs at Zoo Atlanta. We didn't need a youth employment program for our urban community—we simply needed connected neighbors who were willing to be good neighbors.

The same kind of connecting took place among adult neighbors who were employed at larger companies with decent benefits. When they shared with their less-connected neighbors the opportunities that were available in the larger economy, prosperity in the community edged upward.

As I've stated, reneighboring is essential to restoring health to deteriorating communities. Simply sharing space, however, is not enough: occupying adjacent housing in a culturally diverse neighborhood is not the same as becoming a good neighbor. If transformation is to take place, genuine relationships have to be forged. Relocaters and remainers have to join together in addressing the challenges of the community. They must enter into each other's lives, raising their children together, organizing crime watches on their street, serving together on the PTA. *Sharing life* is what transforms a community.

That sort of sharing doesn't just happen; it's not the automatic result of living side by side, as one church discovered. A decade or so after the initial CCDA relocation surge had gained momentum, relocaters in that large downtown congregation—one that had inspired scores of members to move into a high-crime neighborhood adjacent to the church—began having serious second thoughts. The pastor and his married son had led the way and purchased homes in the target community. Other members had quickly followed. But after nearly ten years of "neighboring," there was little appreciable improvement in the neighborhood. Drug houses still operated; the schools were still failing; break-ins were still commonplace. The pastors and their relocated followers were showing signs of battle fatigue.

"I'm not sure this is working," the pastor confided. As a matter of fact, both he and his son were already making plans to move out. After all their concerted efforts to "reach out" to their new neighbors, very few of those folks were coming to church and none had joined. "These people have very little interest in the gospel," he lamented.

A red flag began to wave in the back of my mind. The pastor assured me that neighborhood people were participating in the programs the church had initiated in the community—ESL classes, teen pregnancy counseling, and financial assistance with budgeting. But these activities weren't yielding conversions, he said—at least not the kind that led to active church involvement.

What baffled me was why the community was showing no significant signs of improvement after nearly ten years and one hundred–plus new mission-motivated neighbors. With that much fresh energy, capacity, vitality, and commitment, the neighborhood should have been dramatically changed by this time. I understood why lower-income minority neighbors weren't attending this upper-income white church. It was simply not a good cultural fit. New wineskins needed to be fashioned from the language, customs, history, and values of these diverse people. But that was a church planting issue, not a community transformation issue.

"Are you involved in the life of the community?" I asked, probing a bit deeper. The pastor nodded, reiterating the programs the church was providing for the neighborhood. I pressed further. "But are you and other church leaders actively engaged in community life—the neighborhood association, the PTA, the local crime watch?"

"Too much politics," the pastor explained. "All these people do is bicker over who's in charge and who's going to get city grant money."

Now *that* I understood! Community politics can get ugly. But withdraw from the fray? No, that's precisely where redemptive influences are needed most! Did these church people not see that their active leadership was key to the reclamation of a neighborhood turned ugly from callous neglect and petty turf guarding?

And then it dawned on me. This church was operating out of a personal-salvation, church-centric theology. No wonder the community hadn't been impacted by these new neighbors! Their primary strategy was to invite the "locals" to church, where they could hear and receive the gospel message, engage in good biblical learning, and be nurtured in the life of the body. Becoming neighbors and providing programs were simply means, as these relocaters saw it, to the ends that lost souls would be saved and the church would grow. Who could fault such solidly spiritual aims? Who could have predicted that a strategy so rightly motivated would prove to be so ineffective?

The missing ingredient in their outreach approach was a shalom doctrine. Their saved-lost dichotomy of personal salvation didn't take into account God's desire also to redeem fallen systems, to heal alienated relationships, to confront injustices. Absent from their understanding of evangelism was an active seek-the-peace-of-the-city theology. Without a vision for the transformation of the neighborhood, a vision that included every aspect of community life—safety, education, economics, and politics, as well as spiritual vitality— these new neighbors-with-an-agenda were seen as more of a threat than a blessing.

Reconciliation

WHILE THE RELOCATION REQUIRED by reneighboring is the most radical R, reconciliation is generally the most challenging—though also potentially the most rewarding. Living together as diverse neighbors on the same street is different from going to a racially mixed church. When things don't go well at church, when the politics get messy or the sermons turn bland, you can always leave. And most do from time to time. But when things go badly in the neighborhood, it isn't quite so easy to pull up stakes and leave, especially if you own a home there. In some ways, urban community life is more difficult than church life. The diversity is greater, for example. Neighbors may dress in strange attire, eat unusual food, play loud music, have a yard full of old cars, hang out all hours of the night, even speak different languages. But they are all neighbors nonetheless. At some level, they must all coexist. When community works, when the neighborhood is blessed with a leavening of reconcilers, when neighbors join together in common activities (like a block party or a crime watch), the very diversity that would splinter any church gives life richness and flavor.

Community that works can have a corrective impact on even those tempted to operate outside the law. Greg was one of our next-door neighbors when we moved into a mixed-income neighborhood. We soon noticed a steady stream of traffic that stopped by his house when he was home from work. Several of the neighbors voiced concerns about drug transactions, and so we decided to confront Greg. Together, we told him that we weren't willing to take the risk of one of our kids being cut down in the cross-fire of a transaction gone wrong. The business had to stop, we told him, or we would do whatever was within our power to have him removed from the community. It took one twenty-four-hour cycle for the traffic to stop, and it has never returned. Greg has become one of our active neighbors. Community, when it works, can have a reconciling effect.

And this sharing is certainly not a one-way street. Reconciliation involves reaching across the barriers of race, class, and culture, receiving as well as giving, and learning to respect and trust those from whom we have been estranged.

Redistribution

REDISTRIBUTION SOUNDS LIKE . . . well, like a socialist charity tax, doesn't it? But this isn't about taking from the rich to give to the poor. Rather, in CCDA thinking, redistribution bridges the chasms that separate the rich and the poor. Redistribution is the natural outcome of being neighbors in a diverse community. It is neither a doctrine nor a formula. Rather, it is a predictable result of engaging in authentic relationships with those who are different from oneself.

Exchange might be a better word to describe this outcome, because exchange assumes that everyone has something of value to contribute to the life of a community. No one is so broken, so dysfunctional, so disadvantaged that he or she has nothing to offer. The key is believing this, then identifying and engaging the talents that reside within each of our neighbors. It matters not, for example, that my next-door neighbors embrace a different lifestyle than I do. What is important is that they keep an eye on my house when I'm out of town. When my car won't start in the morning, I call my mechanic neighbor, no matter his race or economic status. When my child has a fever or upset stomach, my neighbor, a nurse, is the first person I phone, regardless of her religious affiliation. Even the men who hang out around the fire barrel outside our thrift store add value: their watchful eyes provide a measure of security. And then, of course, I myself have certain resources that are of value to my neighbors—tools to lend, contacts that can lead to employment, a computer for homework assignments. Because we live in proximity to one another—and because we choose to depend on one another—the opportunities for exchange (redistribution) become a normal part of community living. Every one of us is motivated at least by self-interest if not by more noble spiritual values.

Such sharing of talents and resources is more common among the poor than among the more affluent, since sharing is essential for survival when resources are scarce. Those with abundance have less perceived need for others. In mixed-income neighborhoods this difference can prove problematic. Vince, my neighbor who lives in a volunteer-built house across the street, shared with me one day about the struggle he and his wife, Angela, experience as they stand in the rain at the bus stop in the morning and watch my wife, Peggy, and me drive past in our separate cars. It's hard, he told me, to see neighbors who have so much when he and his family have so little.

"Would it be better to live in separate communities where we aren't confronted every day with these inequities?" I asked him.

"Oh, no," Vince responded emphatically. "This is our spiritual work—to not be envious!" The benefits to his family from living in a healthy mixed-income neighborhood, he said, far outweigh the struggles.

My spiritual work, I have to confess, has been learning to share. I grew up in a family and in a culture where self-sufficiency was the normative value. There was little need for sharing. As a matter of fact, it was considered inappropriate to borrow from a neighbor. Every family was responsible for addressing its own needs. Even among our family members, each of us had our own room, our own clothes, and our own "stuff." You didn't get into someone else's things—at least not without permission. So when I relocated to a mixed-income neighborhood, I was not at all prepared to freely lend my lawn mower and my tools—let alone my car—to neighbors, for whom sharing was a normal practice.

The morning I watched Vince and Angela pull away from my house in my late-model Chevy on their way to the coast for a long-delayed honeymoon (with their kids!), I experienced a momentous internal value shift. It was a shift from individual ownership to kingdom stewardship. My possessions, I realized in a very vivid way, were not my own. Though I had been taught all my life about stewardship, it had always been interpreted to and by me in terms of being responsible for the things God had entrusted to my care, an interpretation that actually made it difficult to distinguish stewardship from ownership. The idea of letting go, of allowing others to share in the use and responsibility of my material assets, was as foreign to my thinking as the other two Rs of the CCDA philosophy.

This shift in values has proven, in my case anyway, not to be a one-time event. I've concluded that my spiritual work of letting go of personal ownership may be a lifelong process. And I have learned, too, that redistribution is not one-way charity. It is reciprocal, an honest exchange. It assumes that both parties have something of worth to contribute to the relationship, in surprising and often lasting ways.

Practicing the Three Rs

ONE OF THE BEST examples of reneighboring is Atlanta's East Lake neighborhood. I described its transformation in *Toxic Charity*, but the East Lake model continues to mature and its impact continues to expand around the country. Given the ongoing nature of this community's remarkable transformation, it's worth revisiting here.

In its heyday, East Lake was a suburban playground for Atlanta's affluent, the site of the prestigious East Lake Golf Club that golf legend Bobby Jones called home. But eventually money drifted north out of Atlanta, and the community went into a slow decline, which caused the golf course to slip into disrepair. The final nail in the old course's coffin was the construction of a drab, barracks-style 650-unit public housing project—the deceptively named East Lake Meadows—just outside its gates. With a crime rate eighteen times the national average, East Lake Meadows soon earned a reputation as one of the most desperate, dangerous public housing projects in the nation. Due to its unending gunfire and violence, residents called it Little Vietnam. Mail carriers would not deliver there. Probation officers would not enter without police protection. It was a cancer that infected the entire sur-rounding community.

For years, the city housing authority and nonprofit groups tried to come up with sustainable plans to help East Lake. Nothing ever came of them, however; East Lake remained a notorious neighborhood. Until a Presbyterian businessman named Tom Cousins entered the scene with an inspired idea. Cousins's vision was to restore the old golf course to its 1920s grandeur (complete with Bobby Jones's clubs, trophies, and jackets), recruit wealthy corporate members to join, and use the proceeds to transform the community. A necessary first step was to get rid of the housing project. In its place, Cous-ins proposed a beautifully designed mixed-income apartment community so attractive that any Atlanta citizen, regardless of income level, would desire to live there. Half the apartments would be priced for residents of public housing. It was an au-dacious concept, one that had not been tried before—indeed, one that most considered foolhardy. But Tom was a successful real estate developer, and he wasn't averse to risk. Undeterred, he forged ahead with his plan.

The golf course restoration moved ahead quickly. Fortune 500 CEOs soon joined, and the club landed the prestigious (and lucrative) PGA Tour championship. But that was the easy part. Demolishing and redesigning a government-owned housing project turned out to be a bit more complicated. For starters, the politics were daunting. HUD bureaucrats resisted. Residents of East Lake were suspicious. Everyone, it seemed, had serious doubts about mixing low-income and middle-income households in the same apartment complex.

But Tom was convinced that this was the best way to create a wholesome, hopeful community environment. He believed that people of goodwill, many motivated by faith, would choose to become residents in a diverse community if it were safe, well managed, and replete with high-quality amenities. He was right.

After many months of persistent negotiating and arm-twisting, a complicated agreement was finally signed and the housing project came crashing down. In its place rose an attractive community of garden apartments and townhomes, 542 units in all, clustered around the fairways of the new executive-level golf course. The community was known as the Villages of East Lake.

Half the apartments were occupied by public housing residents and half by market-rate occupants. Original East Lake Meadows residents were given priority to either move back into the new development or select from other subsidized housing options in the city. Unemployed residents agreed to attend training courses that prepared them for entry into the workforce. A resident community chaplain was hired to initiate neighbor-led activities to build wholesome relationships among diverse neighbors.

The results were stunning. Violent crime dropped by 95 percent. Household incomes for public housing residents increased steadily, rising from less than $4,500 when the program began to more than $17,000 by 2012. Educational achievement in the neighborhood grade school went from dead last to the top-performing school in the city. In the old East Lake Meadows grade school, only 5 percent of fifth-graders passed state math standards. In the new Drew Charter School that replaced it, 99 percent of fifth-graders pass. Surrounding property values have risen 334 percent—increasing five times faster than the Atlanta average.

The initiative has spurred more than $200 million in new private investment within a 1.5-mile radius of the development, which goes a long way toward explaining why property values have risen so dramatically. A new Publix supermarket that opened across the street brought into the community new employment opportunities and high-quality food at competitive prices. Low-income residents, once isolated in a dangerous, dead-end poverty compound, now enjoy the benefits common to the majority of Americans—a decent education, achievement-oriented neighbors, economic opportunity, and a safe, hope-filled environment.

The success of East Lake was so striking that the Atlanta Housing Authority decided to tear down all of its twenty-five housing projects and replace them with mixed-income apartment communities. Today, not a single government "poverty compound" remains in the city.

Can we conclude that the poverty needle in the East Lake community has swung in a positive direction? Certainly the influx of several hundred middle-class residents has raised the disposable income level in the area, creating measurable economic impact. But, as we have seen, simply displacing low-income residents and replacing them with higher-income neighbors does not directly address the issue of poverty. The true measure of poverty alleviation is the impact of reneighboring on the lives of the poor. Have the lower-income residents of East Lake developed their personal capacities? Has their motivation to achieve increased? Have they climbed the economic ladder to better jobs? Has self-sufficiency replaced dependency? In The Villages of East Lake, the answer to all of these is a resounding yes!

Can the East Lake model be replicated in other cities? Admittedly, not every city has a famous golf course to resurrect as a cash cow. But most cities have potentially attractive features worth capitalizing on: a riverfront, for example, or a municipal park, or a historic site. With the increasing popularity of in-town living, neighborhoods once thought to be undesirable have a good chance of rebounding simply because of their proximity to downtown.

Given the challenges inherent in implementing the three Rs, it's worth underlining how and why the East Lake model produced such a remarkable turnaround. It was so successful because it focused on six key elements:

1. *Vision.* The driving force that ignited and propelled this venture was a visionary with a deep desire to see lasting transformation take place in a desperate place.

2. *Location.* A central location on a major thoroughfare accessible to downtown made East Lake prime for redevelopment.

3. *Focus.* A concentrated, comprehensive convergence of efforts focused on one defined location gave investors much-needed traction.

4. *Justice.* A mixed-income strategy ensured that lower-income residents, who are often the victims of gentrification, have permanent belonging in a wholesome community.

5. *Safety.* This value tops the list for both rich and poor when considering where they will choose to live. From the beginning, it was a top priority in the East Lake development.

6. *Quality education.* Next to safety, education is a primary attraction for families, especially upwardly mobile families, many of whom will relocate specifically for this reason. It was a key to East Lake's mixed-income success.

These essential elements of the East Lake model can certainly be replicated, if on a smaller scale. As a matter of fact, the very team that transformed East Lake, including Atlanta's former mayor, recently launched Purpose Built Communities, a nonprofit organization formed to support such community redevelopment efforts. The organization offers free expert consultation and practical assistance to any city or group serious about mixed-income community development.

CHAPTER EIGHT

Gentrification with Justice

EDUCATION AND ECONOMIC DEVELOPMENT

MAINLINE DENOMINATIONS ARE STRUGGLING THESE days. Their attendance is declining; their budgets are shrinking; their membership is graying. There is a good bit of hand-wringing at denominational headquarters about how to reverse these trends. Leadership is exploring all manner of innovative ideas that might hold the secret to filling old wineskins with new wine.

I was recently invited to speak at a national convention of one of these aging denominations, one that I have belonged to most of my adult life (and still do). Organizers of the conference figured that a bit of public goading from a seasoned para-church practitioner might spur the denomination toward more cutting-edge ministry. It was worth the risk, they reasoned.

My denomination places a high value on education—education for clergy, for members, and for the poor they serve. It has given birth to some of the nation's finest educational institutions, created top-notch seminaries here and abroad, and initiated quality primary and secondary schools in some of the poorest places on earth. It was no surprise, then, that education would be a rallying cry for the World Mission division as its leaders issued the challenge to conference attendees to support a campaign to alleviate poverty. The lack of education, they said, is a root cause of poverty; the statistics were undeniable, they declared with conviction. Their poverty alleviation strategy: 1,001 new students freed from the shackles of poverty in 2014 through educational scholarships.

The small-group workshop I led on poverty alleviation drew mission leaders and pastors who were willing (some even eager) to consider new ways of serving the poor. Even with that receptive audience, it was controversial enough. But my plenary luncheon address, intended by conference organizers to support their poverty alleviation plan, met serious resistance. I simply could not agree with the campaign theme that education was *the way* out of poverty. Not for a poor community. I could certainly affirm that education is an important door of opportunity for individuals, yes; essential, no doubt. But it is not sufficient to lift a village or a people out of poverty.

As I waded into the topic, it was obvious that the reaction was mixed. I heartily agreed with my denominational friends that education is vitally important to the alleviation of poverty.

The statistics are clear—education and earnings are closely correlated. But education detached from a community development vision becomes an individualistic pursuit. I'm not at all sure that the goal of 1,001 new students in 2014 will reduce poverty by more than 1,001 individuals (and perhaps some of their families). Without a plan for the economic development of the communities from which these students come, education will not move the poverty needle.

So how do we connect the two—education and economic development?

Inferior education is both a symptom and a cause of poverty. Improving the quality of education opens the door to an outside world of opportunity. *Outside* is the operative word here. When a ghetto child or the daughter of an Appalachian coal miner or the son of a sub-Saharan farmer chooses to leave home to pursue an education, parents know in their hearts that the chances are slim that their child will ever return home. This was not an issue my audience was prepared to engage, however. A few gave understanding nods, but most seemed unsettled by the additional layers of complexity I was introducing into their campaign. This group understood education—not community economic development. The discussion was tabled, the meeting adjourned; and the education strategy was later adopted.

Education is the ticket out. Unless (and this is a big *unless*) there is a compelling reason to return. Lawndale Community Church has successfully created such a vision in the hearts and minds of its young members. Located in one of Chicago's roughest neighborhoods, Lawndale is a *community* church—both in policy and in practice. Thirty years ago, when the church was just forming, the unchurched street kids who comprised the majority of its organizing members decided that only neighborhood residents could join. One might question their wisdom and motives, but their decision anchored the church in the community. Over time it would prove to be the most significant decision the church ever made.

As its teenage members matured into young adults and pursued opportunities in the broader Chicago economy, they wanted to stay connected to the church. For many, it had become the center of their social life. And, though their growing financial capacity allowed them to "move on up" to a better location, their desire to remain part of the church community kept them in Lawndale. This meant that the leadership-depleted neighborhood began to retain some of its best and brightest residents. Those youth who aspired to attend college were offered scholarships by the church in exchange for their involvement as counselors in summer camps for neighborhood children. This implanted in the imaginations of those college-goers a vision for what their neighborhood could become. Many were inspired to continue their involvement into adulthood. Over the years, Lawndale Community Church has become a powerful agent of transformation, developing hundreds of housing units, creating countless jobs, encouraging entrepreneurship, providing training of all sorts, and operating the largest private health and fitness center in the city—all while instilling a vision for their community within a new generation of youth.

The pilot project that we initiated in Nicaragua, which we'll look at in greater detail in chapter 9, has been attempting a similar thing—with some encouraging results. In 2011, after five years of on-the-ground community economic development work, the impact of the Opportunity Nicaragua project was obvious. The project helped set up a self-sustaining food-processing plant to buy, sell, and ship produce for several hundred farmers. The project also introduced several strains of hybrid yucca that yielded growers substantially higher profits. Additionally, the project developed new markets for hibiscus flowers (for tea) and tamarind seeds (for jam and juices), which enabled farmers to diversify their cash crops. It was apparent that the Pacific south region of Nicaragua was a prime location for agricultural expansion.

During this same five-year period, tourism in Nicaragua began to bud. Nicaragua is a natural eco-wonderland. The Pacific Rim's volcanic "Ring of Fire" runs through the country, accenting the tropical landscape with both active and inactive volcanoes. The country's Atlantic and Pacific coastlines offer breathtaking views and unspoiled beaches. Wildlife abounds. The only reason that this lush, picturesque land is not flourishing as a destination vacation spot is its turbulent revolutionary history. But today, acceptable political stability has returned. A handful of luxury hotels and resorts have appeared, signaling the beginning of new opportunity for this poorest of Central American countries.

Two unexploited opportunities—agriculture and tourism. Two industries with untapped potential sufficient to bring prosperity to an entire nation. But there's a problem. There are no schools in the region to prepare young people to capitalize on these opportunities. Government schools are substandard. Ninety percent of the students drop out before graduation, while nearly a third never attend school at all.

It became obvious that if the Opportunity Nicaragua project was to get serious about alleviating poverty, it would have to take the long view. Five years of community economic development work had only scratched the surface. To have lasting impact, the board realized, an educational ladder had to be created to give the emerging generation an opportunity to ascend. Which is why we decided to make the pilot project permanent. In 2012 we launched Emprendedora Technical High School.

Emprendedora is a technical high school that offers degrees in tourism and agriculture. Students get hands-on experience working either in a first-class eco-hotel, one that was developed by Christian business investors, or on the experimental farm located on the school grounds. They learn by doing. Tourism majors work alongside chefs, hotel managers, and maintenance directors, learning every aspect of the hospitality business. Students majoring in agriculture raise chickens, sell eggs, produce honey, and grow organic vegetables. They currently have twenty-four varieties of yucca under cultivation on the farm; and, working closely with the food-processing plant, they conduct research on such things as starch content, nutritional value, drought resistance, and fluctuating market values. The students' work pays for much of their tuition, which allows the school to be self-sustaining. When students graduate, they are prepared for gainful employment in local industries, ready for college, or equipped to start their own businesses.

Education and economic development are inseparable partners. They belong together.

Education: Key to Poverty Alleviation?

PAUL TUDOR JONES IS a billionaire with a big heart. His Robin Hood Foundation is New York's largest poverty-fighting charity. Over the past two and a half decades, he has raised more than a billion dollars from two hundred thousand New Yorkers. Every penny he's collected has gone directly to the front lines of the city's most effective nonprofits. But Jones is no softhearted philanthropist. He's a hard-driving hedge-fund manager, dead-serious about return on investment. And he expects no less from every one of the five hundred nonprofits he supports. Each one must have a solid business plan with clear goals and objectives, and a tracking system for measurable results. Those that fail he defunds. His foundation staff are highly competent analysts and accountants who conduct "best practices" research, provide training and support to grant recipients, and ensure accountability. Foundation overhead is covered by board members so that every donor dollar goes directly to addressing human need. Within the philanthropic world, the Robin Hood Foundation is a model of excellence.

Jones believes that education is the key to eliminating poverty. His research shows clearly that education level has a high statistical correlation with earning potential. Thus, if children are to emerge from poverty, they must receive a quality education. Jones's first venture into this arena was inspired by wealthy businessman Gene Lang, who "adopted" a Harlem high school class in 1986, promising every student a full college scholarship upon graduation. The experiment was a well-publicized success. Jones tried to replicate the approach in a Brooklyn middle school class, but it failed. The reason, Jones concluded, was that he didn't begin at an early enough age.

His second attempt, in 2004, was Excellence Boys Charter School, a K–8 all-male school housed in a former crack house in a rough part of Brooklyn. This time the results were more encouraging. Math and science scores came in significantly higher than average, while reading scores were slightly above average. Jones was encouraged.

In a 2013 *60 Minutes* interview, Jones was questioned about the poverty rate in New York City. He was asked whether the billion-dollar Robin Hood investment had improved the city's poverty level. Was the infusion of huge sums of charitable cash into the city's best charities and most promising public schools having any measurable effect on the alleviation of poverty? "No, not really," Jones admitted. And he's right: poverty is still holding at 20 percent, virtually unchanged in twenty-five years. "I'm investing in *futures*," the hedge-fund philanthropist offered as justification. Maybe it would take another generation or two to see results, he implied.

Or not. Education, like other poverty-fighting strategies we've considered in earlier chapters, may be essential to the health of a community, but it is not sufficient. The same is true of responsibly run social service programs. They may be necessary safety nets, but they do not alleviate poverty. You cannot educate or serve a community out of poverty. Unless the parents of schoolchildren have jobs that enable them to adequately provide for their families, no amount of public or private subsidy will lift them from dependency. Good services may bring Meals on Wheels to seniors, offer Boys & Girls Clubs for kids, and establish daycare centers for infants, but such services alone will not move the needle. The best that education can deliver to the children of a dependent community is a ticket out. A community will never become healthy unless it is economically viable. And that means upwardly mobile neighbors with decent jobs.

Look at what happened in my backyard in the early years of this new century, when city leaders became convinced that improving the test scores in Atlanta Public Schools (APS) was more important than strengthening healthy community life. Political leaders on both sides of the aisle, the downtown business association, the philanthropic community—*everyone* was rallying around the new APS superintendent, Dr. Beverly Hall, who was confident she could lead the troubled system out of a relentless downward spiral that had dragged it to the bottom of the nation's urban education barrel. And, by all accounts, she was delivering! Standardized test scores were on the rise, a new school board of respected leaders had been elected, and substantial corporate and foundation dollars were being invested to bolster lagging property tax revenues. An optimism that hadn't been felt for decades was in the air. Dr. Hall was getting the job done. Atlanta, the entire city predicted, would soon become a national model for turning around urban education.

That is, until a couple of investigative reporters took a closer look, later in the decade, at the phenomenal reversal in student academic performance. The dramatic increase seemed improbable to these reporters—the gains reported by some schools were so great as to be statistically impossible. An unwelcome exposé made front-page news in the Atlanta paper, which ignited an investigation by the governor's office. One hundred and eighty-five APS administrators and teachers were eventually implicated in test cheating schemes in forty-four schools. Some pleaded guilty; others took probation in exchange for their cooperation. Still others were cleared due to insufficient evidence. In 2013 a grand jury handed down a massive indictment charging thirty-five of them with rack-eteering, theft (in the form of taking undeserved bonuses), and conspiring to change students' answers on federally mandated curriculum tests.

A correspondent for the *Atlanta Journal-Constitution* covering the plea hearings reported the drama this way: "One educator after another—some breaking down in tears—said they were told test score targets had to be reached, even when it was common knowledge this could not be accomplished without changing students' scores or giving them correct answers. Excuses would not be tolerated, they said." Thirteen of the accused, including Dr. Hall, maintained their innocence and went to trial. Eleven were convicted. Dr. Hall, whose trial had been temporarily delayed due to treatment for stage 4 breast cancer, passed away in early 2015, before her trial ended.

The dream of high-quality public education that ignited so much hope in Atlanta is now gone. A new superintendent has been hired, but few people express optimism that APS will do more than maintain the status quo. Why is it that APS and so many other urban school systems across the country are delivering substandard education? Why do half or more of our public school students drop out before they graduate? Our public education system was once the pride of our nation—the melting pot that forged streams of immigrants from around the globe into a workforce that created the most successful nation in history. What went wrong?

I'm neither a historian nor an educator, so I do not pretend to have an adequate answer to what is a very complex question. What I do have, however, is firsthand knowledge of the educational decline in one American city—Atlanta. And I am witnessing from the front lines what I believe could be the beginning of the turnaround of that system.

What causes me to be optimistic? Two things: (1) gentrification and (2) a younger generation of professionals who view diversity as a good thing. Before the cheating scandal, when Atlanta was euphoric about our (fabricated) educational improvements, I asked Dr. Hall why she placed so much emphasis on raising test scores and spent so little effort on recruiting the children of the new wave of educationally motivated parents moving into Atlanta. Why, I asked, would APS not invest in creative alternatives, such as specialized charter schools and high-achieving academies, to draw achievers back into the public system? I had no way of knowing at the time that improved test scores, not actual educational achievement, were the measure by which educators were being evaluated and rewarded.

How to Gentrify with Justice

IN RECENT YEARS GENTRIFICATION has become the norm in American cities large and small. Neighborhoods that were once neglected have suddenly become attractive. Proximity to revitalized urban centers and the affordability of real estate understandably appeal to an upwardly mobile younger generation. But does this move the poverty needle? Gentrification certainly increases the income level of once-neglected neighborhoods. So, in that sense, yes, it does a bit—but only at the expense of the poor who are displaced in the process (as we saw earlier).

Gentrification alone, as we understand it, is not a legitimate means to move the poverty needle. Gentrification is successful in alleviating poverty only when it is part of an intentionally planned strategy of mixed-income redevelopment that protects the interests of the poor. *That* sort of gentrification can have a direct and positive impact on poverty.

When low-income residents are included in the planning, implementation, and ongoing life of their reviving neighborhood, they become the beneficiaries rather than the victims of gentrification. An influx of affluent neighbors attracts new businesses—restaurants, grocery stores, and banks, among others. That means new job opportunities, improved services, and competitive prices that benefit all residents, especially those with limited incomes. Political leaders begin to take note, which leads to access to public funds, which in turn leads to significant changes in a neighborhood's infrastructure: improved police protection, stepped-up code enforcement, paved potholes, repaired sidewalks. Educated neighbors insist on quality schools; and if the public system can't deliver, they create alternatives that can, as we saw in the East Lake example. The net effect of *shared* community benefits—more employment opportunities, better food prices, better housing, better education—actually does move the poverty needle in a positive direction. This is gentrification with justice.

For years it has been obvious to everyone in my neighborhood that the public schools were not delivering the quality of education that our children—any of our children, rich or poor—deserved. The obsession with test scores, which has been a subject of media criticism for years (and which eventually exploded in Atlanta, as we just saw), seemed always to be more of a distraction than a motivation. The tipping point came in our community when Chris and Rebecca Gray, co–executive directors of FCS, adopted two little orphan girls from China. Chris and Rebecca, both with doctorates, were determined to create a high-quality charter school strong enough to draw in the "gentry"—but a school also committed enough to raise the performance of low-income students.

In spite of resistance from APS hierarchy, in 2006 the Grays forged ahead to create Wesley International Academy, an International Baccalaureate school with gender-separate classes, dual language courses (English and Chinese), and a full after-school enrichment program, including music lessons, dance classes, homework assistance, and a variety of other stimulating activities. Although APS would not permit quotas to achieve an economic balance, they did agree to allow targeted marketing. The result was an enrollment of 60 percent middle- and upper-income children and 40 percent lower-income children. Priority was given to neighbors who lived in the community.

Wesley International Academy, the first of its kind in Atlanta, was intriguing enough to attract résumés from educators all over the country and from as far away as mainland China. With freedom to hire faculty and set policies that served the interests of students rather than the tenure of teachers, Wesley immediately became an environment of innovation and vigorous learning. Student performance soared to the top of APS schools. The PTA won state awards for parent participation. To ensure a quality educational experience for all their students, Wesley offered supplemental tutoring so that the bar remains high for students from less advantaged backgrounds.

When the city of Atlanta hosted Chinese dignitaries to encourage international trade, Wesley was on the tour. The Chinese guests were impressed to hear American schoolchildren speaking Mandarin clearly and with perfect diction. Wesley's Chinese faculty made sure of that. By the time Wesley students graduate from college, Mandarin will doubtless be the second language of international trade. A world of opportunity will be open to those who are fluent in both Chinese and English.

Education may well be an individual's ticket out of a depressed community, but a quality neighborhood-oriented school like Wesley is a community-builder. It attracts new leadership into the area—specifically, educated parents who want to move to an in-town community and will invest in its revitalization so long as there are good educational options for their children. At the same time, a first-rate school provides an inducement for existing lower-income residents to remain.

Wesley is one example of why I remain optimistic about public education. Gentrification, a new norm in our society, is rearranging the demographics of our metropolitan areas. The gentry gravitating into the city bring with them educational values that demand quality schools. They embrace diversity. They do not want to sacrifice quality, but they are quite willing to expend effort for the sake of inclusion. Mixed-income living is attractive to them, as is mixed-income education. For city schools, this is a hopeful sign.

Perhaps the effects of the APS cheating scandal will not be as disastrous as Atlantans first feared. The experience peeled back the lid on an entrenched bureaucracy that had focused more on tenure than on transformation. Perhaps now, with a younger, visionary superintendent at the helm, the educational climate will become more conducive to innovation, more community-friendly, more responsive to an increasingly educated population. At the very least, I hope that our new leader will focus less on attendance rates, dropout prevention, and test scores, and more on practical vocational preparation that directly connects students to jobs in the essential trades and services that make the city run. An education that leads to decent employment is the only kind of education that makes any sense.

CHAPTER NINE

For-Profit Missions

INTERNATIONAL DEVELOPMENT

IT's ONE THING TO REVITALIZE a local neighborhood already poised for gentrification. It's quite another to stimulate economic growth (that is, create decent jobs) in an underdeveloped country where the economy is on life support. There are many reasons for persistent poverty in places such as Haiti, sub-Saharan Africa, and Central America. Natural disasters, war, unstable governments, and aid, to name just a few. But in almost any environment, no matter how troubled or destitute, there is unharnessed potential for development. Years of dependency-producing charity and misguided aid may have significantly weakened a country's self-sufficiency, yet among every people there resides a divine impulse that aspires to rise to full potential. More nonprofit services, including orphanages, schools, and medical clinics—as important as they are—will not enable a people to rise out of poverty. Only living-wage jobs can move the poverty needle—jobs that local residents create through their own hard work and ingenuity, and jobs produced by for-profit businesses created by outside investors and operators.

Fishing, farming, mining, and manufacturing are the classic wealth-producing activities in any land. In developing countries, the poor scratch out a living through microbusinesses that rely on these activities. Catch enough fish to feed your family and on a good day sell some extra at the market. Plant enough yucca for an adequate diet but not enough to truck to the big city. Produce enough handwoven baskets to sell at the straw market but not enough to export. However, there is only so much that an informal hand-to-mouth economy can yield. Thus microenterprises enable people to survive but not to thrive. They are jobs, yes—but not jobs that alleviate poverty.

In underdeveloped countries, there is virtually no middle class. At the top are the very wealthy, who own the large national and international companies. At the bottom are the very poor, who scratch out a living from the land or from roadside microbusinesses. The "missing middle" is small to midsize businesses—the kinds of enterprises that generate the lion's share of jobs and wealth in *our* country. That business class in underdeveloped countries is virtually nonexistent.

But that's what the millions in microloans raised among socially conscious contributors are for, right? Don't *they* move the poverty needle? Actually, no. For one thing, most of these small loans to peasants end up as consumer debt, not business investment. With the flood of microlenders that has entered this market in recent years, borrowers are able to obtain credit from multiple sources. As with credit-card debt, borrowers use these high-interest loans to purchase all manner of consumer items. The amount actually going to expand microenterprises is small, and rapidly dwindling.

Even legitimate microbusiness loans, however, don't enable microentrepreneurs to emerge from poverty. It's a quantum leap to graduate from making a few dozen loaves of bread in a small wood-burning oven to owning and operating a commercially viable bakery. Very few uneducated peasants are equipped to tackle the complexities of a medium-size bakery (or any medium-size business). The list of requirements is long. Commercial facilities and automated equipment are needed. Competencies are required in accounting, inventory control, health regulations, government reporting, personnel management, packaging, and marketing, to name but a few of the many hurdles.

There is no lack of native intelligence; the scarcity is in business skills. Without hands-on experience in a business setting, which is where most U.S. business owners get their start, and without adequate capital and access to markets, microbusinesses remain micro. They may allow the poor to survive, but they do not create and build wealth. In order to create wealth, businesses must come to scale.

Successful businesspeople like John Coors understand this. That's why he shifted from his subsidized nonprofit Circle of Light initiative in sub-Saharan Africa (described in chapter 3) to his One Thousand & One Voices investment strategy, which connects wealthy families with African entrepreneurs who need patient capital, influential connections, and industry expertise to grow their businesses. I can't stress it enough: business growth is key to moving the poverty needle.

I discussed in *Toxic Charity* our Opportunity Nicaragua initiative to empower rural farmers to increase their earnings through growing, processing, and marketing yucca. But it's worth repeating here, because this project so clearly illustrates how innovative business ventures can successfully move the poverty needle on a very grassroots level. At first, the Opportunity Nicaragua team attempted to scale up a number of microbusinesses by offering training and larger loans to artisans to expand their handcraft enterprises, as I noted in chapter 2. We tested their products (clothing and accessories, wood bowls, pottery, weavings) on the international market to determine level of demand, made suggestions about color and design, established a website, and developed a thorough marketing strategy. We took samples to the Merchandise Mart in Atlanta, where national retailers assemble each year to place their initial orders for new products on the market.

Filling the larger orders in a timely manner with good quality control proved to be challenging. Artisan hand-skills were specialized, and small cottage operations did not lend themselves to volume production. Hiring and training additional artisans took time, which affected quality control. Furthermore, keeping up with ever-changing market demands required constant innovation and design change. It eventually became apparent that the cottage-industry approach didn't lend itself to a scaled-up, wealth-generating opportunity for hardworking artisans.

So if not handcrafts, what *would* generate profits? we asked ourselves. Could farming be brought to scale? we wondered.

Our community developer, Geralyn Sheehan, observed that yucca, a staple of the local diet (also known as cassava), grew in abundance. She wondered if that crop could be brought to scale and become a source of prosperity for local farmers. There was certainly a market for yucca well beyond local consumption. But in order to ship the crop to Managua and beyond, she found out, yucca would have to be processed and packaged. The sweet potato–like tuber would need to be sorted, washed, dipped in a preservative wax, weighed, and boxed before it could be shipped. Then contracts with wholesalers would have to be negotiated. Still, it was worth a try.

Geralyn first experimented with twelve farmers. The "processing plant" was uncomplicated—a propane tank, a metal vat, and a drying rack in a makeshift pole-barn. But the first harvest yielded good results—good enough to attract forty farmers the next season. And then sixty the following year. Though the yucca-processing operation didn't immediately turn a profit, the farmers were clearly benefiting from the program.

A world-class community developer, Geralyn initiated regular training sessions to acquaint growers with state-of-the-art farming techniques, as well as skills such as budgeting, coordinating harvest schedules, commodity fluctuation, and crop rotation. To enhance communication and planning, Geralyn organized growers into cluster groups, with local farmer-leaders as conveners. Cooperative relationships grew. Leadership emerged. Discussions soon stretched beyond agriculture into family life. Housing improvements and children's education became part of the agenda. To Geralyn, these were important signs that healthy community development was indeed occurring.

As earnings increased, so did the number of farmers. This, we found out, was both good and bad news. The good news was we were growing the local economy at a grassroots level. The bad news was we were *out*growing our own infrastructure. Geralyn soon realized that the processing plant's little propane tank and vat setup was no longer sufficient. Stainless steel equipment was needed, as well as a permanent building for processing and secure storage. Geralyn knew that she needed a business manager to ensure that the operation continued to grow. She posted the need on the web, and a month later David Kone, a successful bilingual entrepreneur from Alabama, arrived.

After giving himself a crash course on yucca, David assessed the situation with an eye toward growth and profitability. If local farmers were to continue to increase their yield, he realized, they would have to shift from a utilitarian grade of yucca to a hybrid strain. This new yucca was more nutritious, but it was also more time-consuming and costly to produce. The switch would require purchasing different seed and changing the farmers' traditional planting techniques. For those farmers willing to take the risk, David arranged agricultural loans. By the next harvest, their profits had increased dramatically. For the first time, the processing plant was breaking even.

Meanwhile, David continued to research state-of-the-art processing equipment. Using his findings, he designed a plant large enough to accommodate four hundred growers. By the end of his second year on the job, three hundred farmers were growing the more profitable variety of yucca, and the processing plant was turning a profit. Not only were farmers improving their earnings, but the plant was employing more than sixty workers.

The new hybrid yucca produced splendid tubers, but the farmers were concerned about the sizable number of small and misshapen tubers that grew on the plant's root system. Although the yucca's grade-A tubers brought a good price at market, these smaller tubers—nearly two-thirds of the plant's yield—were nearly worthless, according to the local farmers, useful only to feed hogs and cows. Surely there must be some way to recover value from this waste product, David reasoned. Which required more research!

David discovered that the starch content in yucca, if reduced to powder form, was useful in all manner of applications, from animal feed to glue to cosmetics. The only problem was, to convert near-worthless surplus into a marketable commodity required a press, a grinder, and a drying system. And a buyer, of course. Fortunately, an international conglomerate called Cargill, the parent company of Purina, operated a large plant a few miles away. They showed great interest in David's yucca-flour idea. The quality would have to be high, of course, and the volume worth the effort. David was convinced that additional investment in more equipment was worth the gamble.

Indeed it was. By the end of David's third year in Nicaragua—year six of the entire Opportunity Nicaragua project at that site—the processing plant was serving four hundred farmers, shipping their grade-A yucca to markets as far away as California, and selling tons of flour to Cargill.

The economy of the region continued to show visible signs of prosperity—tractors replacing oxen, pickups instead of horses, dry metal roofs instead of leaky thatch. But for David, this was only the beginning. He is currently expanding the yucca-processing business to serve one thousand farmers, as well as setting up additional processing options so that farmers can continue to diversify their crops.

Scale. It moves the needle.

Is Business Development Enough?

WHILE IT WAS VERY exciting to see farmers increasing their earnings, jobs being created, and the processing plant turning a profit, Geralyn and David started to experience a bit of tension. David tended to measure success by the numbers—number of farmers participating, yield per acre, volume of produce processed, production cost per ton, commodity price fluctuation, return on investment, and, of course, bottom-line profitability. Geralyn, on the other hand, measured success in terms of human development: Is the community coming together? Is healthy leadership emerging? Is the capacity to plan and execute important community goals growing? Are aspirations rising above day-to-day survival? Is self-sufficiency increasing? Is the quality of life improving? David and Geralyn understood well the importance of both wealth creation and human development. And they were committed to doing both.

Both David and Geralyn knew that this dual approach was crucial if the community was to thrive. Both of them embraced the value of *holistic* community economic development. Each was a capable leader with exceptional skills. But they naturally drifted toward different emphases. Therein lay the tension.

It is a necessary tension. A creative tension. One that maintains balance. Without this tension, David (and those filling his role in other projects around the world) might focus most of his time and energies on business development. Community capacity building could drift down on his priority list. Without this tension, Geralyn (and colleagues who share her passion) might invest her best creative energies in organizing cooperative projects that enhance community potential and well-being. Since developing cooperatives of microentrepreneurs is far less complicated than growing a midsize for-profit business, her economic development efforts could skew toward microenterprise. But for-profit and nonprofit drivers are *both* needed if people in poverty are to emerge in healthy ways. Geralyn and David are both needed.

Jim Heerin, an Atlanta lawyer with a good head for business, understands this tension intuitively. When a client brought Jim some legal work on a proposed new business plan several decades ago, it caught his interest. There was a growing market for shrimp in the United States, Jim learned, most of which was harvested by shrimp boats along the East Coast. His client wanted to construct a series of saltwater ponds along the coast of Florida, where he could harvest shrimp domestically. If his client's calculations were accurate, the scheme could generate attractive profits.

As lawyers sometimes do, particularly those with business instincts, Jim became personally involved in the venture. First as attorney, then as investor, and, in the end, as president. The company would become known as Sea Farms. Early experiments in the Florida Keys proved less than ideal due to fluctuations in temperature and to environmental constraints. After extensive research, the company selected Honduras as an alternative location: its Pacific region offered an ideal climate, ample and affordable land, and a cooperative political environment. The company hired workers to dig a series of ponds and build a processing plant outside the town of Choluteca.

Jim spent the next two decades commuting back and forth to Honduras. Sea Farms emerged as a frontrunner in the booming pond-raised shrimp industry. Though its product was originally marketed to American consumers, Sea Farms quickly found a place in the global market. By the time Jim retired, it was the largest supplier of shrimp in the Western hemisphere, with sixteen thousand acres of land leased for shrimp production.

And the impact of Sea Farms on the local population? The business created fifteen thousand jobs in the Choluteca area, plus a plethora of ancillary jobs and businesses in local stores, banks, and bus services. Skill development, educational advances, and infrastructure improvements were needed investments that served both the company and the community. A mutually beneficial partnership with Solidarity, a Central American labor union, provided health insurance for employees, bus service for workers, and productive communication between the workforce and management. The regional GDP increased dramatically. Today, Sea Farms is one of the most profitable companies in Honduras, a wealth generator whose ownership is shared between U.S. and Honduran stockholders.

Jim has done well and done good at the same time. He derives great satisfaction from the investment of his best years in a business that allowed many people—including himself—to flourish. But when I asked him if he considered his work a ministry, he appeared puzzled. Jim is a Christian. His faith is important to him. He certainly believes that loving God and loving neighbor are important teachings. But he has never viewed his work as *ministry*. Ministry is what churches and religious nonprofits do, in his view. Not businesses. His life as a businessman was fulfilling because his work was both challenging and profitable. Treating his employees well, providing living wages and good benefits, contributing to the prosperity of the regional economy—these were simply smart business practices. Ethical, but not spiritual.

Like so many other businesspeople, Jim has never heard a sermon on the spiritual gift of wealth creation. He has sat through many sermons on stewardship—what to do with his wealth. But for some reason, pastors (who should understand God's designs for an abundant and fruitful earth) neglect one of the primary creative gifts with which God endowed the human family—namely, the ability to create wealth. As Deuteronomy 8:18 says, "Remember the LORD your God, for it is he who gives you the ability to produce wealth." Somehow this essential gift, the one upon which most every other livelihood depends, has been secularized and stripped of its divine significance. Often denigrated by the religious world as mammon, a corrupter, wealth generation has been consistently warned against, but seldom celebrated. Thus although Jim is a dedicated church attendee and generous contributor, he goes off to his job on Monday unaffirmed by the knowledge that his work is precisely the redemptive activity God designed for him. He pursues his secular career never knowing that it is a truer form of ministry than most of the religious activities of the church.

How Do We Run For-Profit Missions?

WHAT CAN WE LEARN from Jim's work in Honduras? What does the Opportunity Nicaragua experiment teach us? For one thing, if we're concerned about moving the poverty needle, it will take more than community development and microenterprise. It will require for-profit, wealth-generating business creation. A nonprofit approach to serving the poor simply cannot raise them out of poverty. It may improve conditions, may enable them to survive at a higher level, but it will not enable them to thrive. Wealth-creating businesses are essential to the creation of stable, well-paying jobs that provide disposable income and allow families to save and invest for their future. Without profitable enterprises, poor people remain poor. They may work very hard to scratch out an existence, but their aspirations remain shackled to survival needs.

Of course, businesses can be for better or for worse. Not every business is a blessing to its employees or its community. There are other foreign-owned sweatshop factories that employ thousands of Nicaraguans at pitifully low wages, and in tax-free zones that exempt them from business and property taxes. Poor wages are better than no wages at all, the government figures—even if no benefits accrue to improved schools, paved roads, or public sanitation. Like the worst types of toxic charity, this kind of bottom-line-only business keeps people in poverty, lures them away from the land, and, when the factory owners depart in pursuit of even cheaper labor, leaves them more destitute than before the jobs arrived. Business without a moral, ethical foundation isn't liberating; it enslaves people in the perpetual cycle of poverty.

The good news, of course, is that the Western church has an abundance of wealth-producing members with the capacity *and the values* to create for-profit businesses that can move the poverty needle in service of the world's poor. Our pews are full of high-capacity businesspeople who have financially supported mission work (especially mission trips) but have not been personally challenged to invest their greatest talent: making money. Further, there is an emerging generation of bright young entrepreneurs whose spirits and imaginations are being drawn toward social enterprise. They seem more driven to make a difference than make a buck. These ethical wealth generators have the potential to permanently impact the world's poverty cultures. Their pragmatic, hard-nosed business efforts, built upon a relational, capacity-building community development foundation, offer promising outcomes to a world stagnating with softhearted service providers.

Is it reasonable to expect that the Western church could recruit from its members enough committed and skilled economic missionaries (people like Geralyn and David) to make an impact sufficient to move the poverty needle in the struggling nations of this world? In recent decades, the church has backed away from sending full-time missionaries, replacing them with short-term mission-trippers. The decline is due in part to the high cost of training, transporting, and maintaining American missionaries and their families for extended periods of time. It is far easier to raise funds for short-term mission trips. Given the current volume of mission trips, however, it would seem reasonable to assume that the interest in longer-term service might still be there if it could be done affordably.

Therein lies one of the benefits of *economic* missionaries. They don't require ongoing subsidies; they are self-sustaining by the very nature of their endeavor. Yes, they may require start-up capital and some investment risk, but if their mission succeeds, they will earn sufficient income to cover their own salary and living expenses, plus generate income for those they serve.

Why does the thought of sending missionaries to create wealth seem so strange to us? Is it because we've been told all our lives that we cannot possess both riches and righteousness? After all, we are cautioned in Matthew 6:24, "You cannot serve God and money"; in Matthew 19:24, "It is easier for a camel to go through the eye of a needle than for a rich person to enter the kingdom of God"; and, perhaps most famously, in 1 Timothy 6:10, "The love of money is a root of all kinds of evils." It's no wonder that we find it odd to mix missionaries and money.

Perhaps, too, we have been jaded by the sweatshop stories we have heard about oppressive business owners who underpay and overwork their employees. Or perhaps it's the traditional image we hold of the missionary—that is, a person who lives a life of self-sacrifice and eschews personal prosperity. Whatever the reasons, the time has come to create a new image for the missionary.

Until we do, we will not see the poor enjoy the fullness of shalom. It is time to reexamine our perceptions of wealth and to realign our thinking with the divine design of shalom: peace and prosperity for all of God's family.

CONCLUSION

CAN WE REALLY MOVE THE poverty needle? More fundamentally, do we really *want* to see the poor of our world thrive? Some folks are not too sure. When I speak to church groups around the country, I frequently get pushback when I describe economic development as true mission work. My more conservative evangelical brothers and sisters view personal evangelism as the ultimate act of love, and building churches as the highest form of mission work. Conversion is for them the dominant driver of missions. According to their theology, God is primarily concerned about saving souls. For my mainline church friends, on the other hand, showing compassion to the poor is a primary motivator—building latrines, digging wells, painting orphanages, serving in medical clinics. In their belief system, God is concerned about all of creation, especially the poor; therefore, so should we be.

All these church groups have one thing in common, though their approaches may vary. They all want their efforts to be ultimately beneficial to those they serve. The motivation behind their service is genuine.

But do they, do we, really want the poor to *thrive*?

"If the poor become prosperous, isn't there a danger that they will be lured into materialism and self-centeredness, and forget about God?" This question, posed more often than you might think, generally comes from spiritually confident Americans who are blind to their own materialism and self-centeredness. But the question is telling. It reflects an unspoken ambivalence about wealth that is shared by many who enjoy the excesses of the American dream. Even though we have more than our share of the world's wealth (though never quite enough), we still can't help wondering if the prosperity of other people (say, the Chinese) will cost us our place of global prominence and privilege. So mine is an honest question: Do we really want the poor to *thrive*?

Conducting tours for concerned suburbanites through my inner-city neighborhood is a routine part of my PR and fundraising responsibilities for our nonprofit organization. Visitors expect to see boarded-up houses, trash-strewn vacant lots, dangerous-looking drug dealers hanging out on street corners. So when I drive visitors down attractive streets with nicely landscaped bungalows, past my house with rockers on the wide front porch, I frequently hear comments such as, "Wow, this is pretty nice—not what I expected in a poor community." To which I reply, "It *should* look nice after thirty years of community development work." My temptation, of course, is to show them the roughest blocks so that they will be moved to become involved with our ministry. The streets that are thriving don't seem to touch hearts in the same way.

We are moved by need. Volunteerism, so huge in our culture, is propelled by meeting need. Does this mean, then, that we have a subliminal motivation to perpetuate poverty so that we always have someone to serve? No, I would never suggest such a thing. It would be unfair, cruel even, to question the motives of caring volunteers who sincerely desire to make a difference in the world. Yet there is *some* reason that we seem content to invest our billions in aid and millions in volunteer work-hours year after year despite seeing almost no positive change in poverty rates. I choose to believe that the reason is a lack of knowledge rather than a lack of heart.

We have been led to believe that our volunteer service alleviates poverty. We have accepted this as fact. This is wrong. If there is one message that this book attempts to drive home, it is that we cannot *serve* people out of poverty. And yet our massive service industry is based upon this false premise. If we truly do want to see the poor thrive, our entire way of thinking, of believing, must change.

So again: Do we really want to see the poor thrive? If we can honestly answer yes to that question, if we can affirm that it is God's desire that all people share in the abundance of our world, that shalom (peace, prosperity, well-being) is the divine design for humanity, then we can embark with confidence on a mission to transform the highly popular yet tragically flawed compassion industry.

Is the alleviation of poverty a realistic goal? With so many million people in our world living on less than two dollars a day, is it conceivable that there is enough goodwill, enough vision, enough generosity among the rich and powerful to eliminate extreme poverty? As I noted in chapter 3, the good news, according to economist Jeffrey Sachs, is that extreme poverty has been reduced by more than half in the past decade. But this is not the result of an increase in humanitarian aid. Rather, it is due to the more competitive trade policies of the two most populous nations on the globe: China and India. These two nations have represented the greatest concentration of global poverty in our lifetime. But because of more progressive government leadership, they have in recent years become major economic powers, creating unparalleled levels of employment for their roughly 2.5 billion inhabitants. We may debate their business ethics, but we cannot deny their dramatic reduction of poverty. If we can learn one thing from these countries, it is that the most effective method of poverty alleviation is economic development. Jobs, whether in emerging countries or in cultures mired in poverty or in ghettos in U.S. inner cities, are the key.

So what is our strategy for increasing prosperity among the people in countries where we send short-term missionaries—

places like sub-Saharan Africa, Central America, and Haiti, as well as urban America? How do we begin to impact such places? Step one is to begin exploring untapped economic opportunities that could be capitalized upon. Let me conclude by recapping some of the more obvious opportunities:

1. *Encourage religious tourism.* Our mission-trippers can bolster the earnings of artisans, craftspeople, and others making a living from the tourist trade by purchasing the products and services that locals provide. By purchasing locally prepared food, by supporting local transportation enterprises (even carriages and rickshaws), by paying for the hospitality of hosts, by hiring locals to serve as tour guides, mission-trippers can infuse a significant amount of capital into the local economy. Entrepreneurial creativity and profits will increase if short-term missionaries become paying customers.

2. *Stop undercutting local businesses by distributing suitcases full of clothing, shoes, candy, and other giveaways.* Donated clothing has put a half million African textile workers out of work. As an example, Ghanaian textile and clothing employment fell by 80 percent from 1975 to 2000 due to the influx of used clothing from Western nations.

3. *Support local self-sufficiency by offering technical training.* A prime example of this strategy is a delegation of Chick-fil-A corporate staff who volunteer consulting time and

travel regularly to Nicaragua to assist a fledgling food-processing plant to develop state-of-the-art management, inventory, and accounting systems.

4. *Provide business loans to entrepreneurs.* Examples: a short-term loan that enabled a peasant family in Guatemala to double the size of their chicken business; a twenty-four-month loan that allowed two sisters in inner-city Atlanta to move their catering business out of their home into a commercial kitchen. By demanding banker-like accountability and charging a reasonable rate of return, lenders make loans a legitimate, dignity-affirming transaction.

5. *Invest with locals in for-profit businesses.* Making money *with* the poor is the highest form of charity. Examples: on a smaller scale, providing start-up capital for a house painter in urban Chicago in exchange for an ownership stake in his LLC; on a larger scale, making a substantial, long-term investment in a midsize African company that accelerates its growth (as John Coors's 1K1V group is doing).

6. *Hire unemployed/underemployed workers.* Take a risk on individuals who are often overlooked. Don't rule out people who come with acceptable references but may have a criminal record, a past history of substance abuse, or a spotty employment history. A bit of research may reveal that such people have undeserved blemishes on their record or have had a genuine change of heart. Given an-

other chance along with some encouragement, they may thrive as employees in a positive work environment and flourish in their family life.

7. *Start for-profit businesses that employ local residents.* Groups like Partners Worldwide are on a mission to end poverty through job creation. Their vision is "to create flourishing economic environments in communities around the world." To date they have created and sustained more than fifty thousand jobs. Yet, as effective as such organizations may be, there is a far greater resource for business creation sitting untapped in the pews of Western churches. Investment trips are needed to ignite the spirit and imagination of our successful business leaders. Investment-worthy business plans must begin to command as much attention and energy as mission trips have in the past. A new generation of economic missionaries—a generation endowed with abundant entrepreneurial capacities—needs commissioning.

The world awaits.

ABOUT THE AUTHOR

Bᴏʙ Lᴜᴘᴛᴏɴ ʜᴀs ɪɴᴠᴇsᴛᴇᴅ over forty years of his life in inner-city Atlanta. In response to a call that he first felt while serving in Vietnam, he left a budding business career to work with delinquent urban youth. Bob, his wife, Peggy, and their two sons sold their suburban home and moved into the inner city where they have lived and served as neighbors among those in need. Their life's work has been the rebuilding of urban neighborhoods where families can flourish and children can grow into healthy adults.

Bob is a Christian community developer, an entrepreneur who brings together communities of resource with communities of need. Through FCS Urban Ministries—a nonprofit organization that he founded—he has developed two mixed-income subdivisions, organized a multiracial congregation, started a number of businesses, created housing for hundreds of families, and initiated a wide range of human services in his community. He is the author of the books *Theirs Is the*

Kingdom; Return Flight; Renewing the City; Compassion, Justice, and the Christian Life; Toxic Charity; and the widely circulated "Urban Perspectives," monthly reflections on the Gospel and the poor. Bob has a Ph.D. in psychology from the University of Georgia. He serves as a speaker, strategist, and inspirer with those throughout the nation who seek to establish God's Shalom in the city.

ABOUT FCS URBAN MINISTRIES

FOR ALMOST FORTY YEARS, Focused Community Strategies (FCS) has been transforming underserved neighborhoods in the heart of Atlanta by providing holistic and innovative community development. FCS, at the invitation of long-term residents, leads a team of skilled partners (organizations and individuals) who have consistently demonstrated the ability to bring positive lasting change to the lives of individuals, as well as to the overall community. Since 2000, FCS has been working in the neighborhood of historic South Atlanta, an underserved community on Atlanta's south side in the 30315 zip code.

FCS initiatives are neighborhood-specific, focusing on a single neighborhood at a time. FCS forms a long-term partnership, and its impact comes through intentional neighboring, strategic planning, dynamic partnership, and innovative program creation. These initiatives are carefully designed to address the long-term needs of the community, while honoring the dignity, culture, and history of the neighborhood.

To learn more about FCS Urban Ministries, please visit their website at www.fcsministries.org or follow them on Facebook or Twitter at @fcsministries.org.

FCS Urban Ministries
PO Box 17628
Atlanta, GA 30316
(404) 627-4304